CLASSICAL CHINESE PRIMER

Workbook

Classical Chinese Primer
Workbook

古文入門作業本

By Sue-mei Wu

吳素美 著

中文大學出版社

Classical Chinese Primer Workbook
By Sue-mei Wu

© **The Chinese University of Hong Kong**, 2007

ISBNs: 978–962–996–340–8
       978–962–996–286–9 (Textbook + Workbook)

THE CHINESE UNIVERSITY PRESS
The Chinese University of Hong Kong
SHA TIN, N.T., HONG KONG
Fax: +852 2603 6692
     +852 2603 7355
E-mail: cup@cuhk.edu.hk
Web-site: www.chineseupress.com

Printed in Hong Kong

Contents

Introduction

This workbook provides exercises for the forty lessons in *Classical Chinese Primer*. The main goals for the workbook are to help learners become more familiar with the main texts in the reader, understand the grammar and writing style of Classical Chinese texts, and be able to recognize the special characteristics of Classical Chinese grammar. Through this training, learners can build up knowledge of Classical Chinese that will help them prepare to eventually read the Chinese classics and historical documents independently.

The language skill most relevant to Classical Chinese is reading. Thus, the slightly pedagogical design of the exercises in the workbook focuses on increasing Classical Chinese literacy. Several types of exercises are provided to help learners systematically develop their Classical Chinese reading skills by learning to recognize the grammatical particularities of Classical Chinese and becoming familiar with the Classical Chinese styles and genre.

The following principles have been used as guidelines in designing the exercises:

(1) Maximize exposure to authentic texts
   The exercises are based on real Classical Chinese texts with the sources indicated. This helps provide learners with more exposure to the authentic texts to broaden their reading scope. Reading the actual texts helps learners have a better grasp of the special characteristics of Classical Chinese, and eventually understand the syntactic structure of the language.

(2) Include ample review and practice of prior materials
   The exercises are based on the texts of both the current and previous lessons. This helps learners review what they have learned.

(3) Work toward and test both achievement and proficiency
   Achievement exercises test how well learners have understood the main texts. Proficiency exercises test how well learners can transfer knowledge and skills acquired from the main texts to new texts.

The following three types of exercises are emphasized throughout the workbook: (1) achievement exercises—which help ensure that learners read and re-read the main text enough to understand it well and retain it in their long-term memories; (2) grammar exercises—which help learners to focus on the grammar points that they learn from the main text and to gain skills that can be applied to the reading of new texts; and (3) reading proficiency exercises.

By going through the exercises for each lesson in the workbook, learners will become more familiar with the main lesson texts and will strengthen their understanding of the vocabulary and grammar of the texts, as well as the special characteristics of Classical Chinese grammar exhibited in them. This will help them to be better readers of Classical Chinese. They will also have a more profound understanding of the history of Chinese language and appreciation for the forty representative Classical Chinese texts which have been selected as the main texts for their historical value, beauty, and influence on later writers.

Ancient Fables (Part 1: A)

一. 寓言選 (上)

(甲) 揠苗助長

✎ I. Text Exercise

Fill in the blanks below. Use one Chinese character for each blank.

1. 以_____無益而_____之者，不耘苗_____也。

2. 其子_____而往視之，苗_____槁矣。

3. 今日病_____，予助苗_____矣！

4. _____之長者，揠_____者也。

5. _____徒無益，而又_____之。

6. 天下之不_____苗長者_____矣！

7. 宋人有_____其苗_____不長而_____之者，_____芒_____歸。

✎ II. Grammar Exercise

Indicate the grammatical function of the word "之" in the following sentences.

1. 宋人有閔其苗之不長而揠之者。

   _____

2. 其子趨而往視之，苗則槁矣。

   _____

3. 天下之不助苗長者寡矣！

   _____

4. 以為無益而舍之者，不耘苗者也。

   _____

5. 助之長者，揠苗者也。

   _____

6. 非徒無益，而又害之。

   _____

✎ III. Rearrangement

With the help of the English translation, rearrange the following Chinese characters in the correct word order.

1. There was a person from the state of Song who felt sorry that his seedlings did not grow, and pulled them up.
   （閔 / 宋人 / 之 / 揠 / 苗 / 有 / 其 / 之 / 而 / 不 / 者 / 長 / 。）

   _____

2. (He) went home tiredly.
   (芒 / 歸 / 然 / 芒 / 。)

   _____

3. (He) spoke to his family.
   (其 / 謂 / 曰 / 人 / 。)

   _____

4. (I) am exhausted today, I have helped the seedlings to grow.
   (病 / 日 / 矣 / 今 / ， / 苗 / 予 / 助 / 矣 / 長 / ！)

   _____

5. His son walked hurriedly and went to see them. The seedlings had all withered.
   (之 / 子 / 視 / 往 / 趨 / 而 / 其 / ， / 苗 / 矣 / 槁 / 則 / 。)

   _____

6. Those of the world who do not assist the seedlings to grow are rare.
   (者 / 天 / 矣 / 之 / 不 / 長 / 助 / 寡 / 苗 / 下 / ！)

   _____

7. Those who neglect things because they consider them to be without benefit are like people who do not weed their seedlings.
   (而 / 之 / 以 / 益 / 舍 / 為 / 者 / 無 / ， / 者 / 苗 / 也 / 耘 / 不 / 。)

   _____

8. Those who rush things are people who pull up their seedlings.
   (長 / 助 / 者 / 之 / ， / 也 / 苗 / 者 / 揠 / 。)

   _____

9. (What they do) is not only useless, but also harms them.
   (徒 / 益 / 非 / 無 / ， / 害 / 之 / 又 / 而 / 。)

╢╟╢╟╢╟╢╟╢╟╢╟╢╟╢╟╢╟ *1* ╢╟╢╟╢╟╢╟╢╟╢╟╢╟╢╟╢╟╢╟

Ancient Fables (Part 1: B)

一. 寓言選（上）

（乙）濫竽充數

✎ I. Punctuation Exercise

Put a dot after each sentence.

齊 宣 王 使 人 吹 竽 必 三 百 人 南 郭 處 士 請 為

王 吹 竽 宣 王 說 之 廩 食 以 數 百 人 宣 王 死 湣

王 立 好 一 一 聽 之 處 士 逃

✎ II. Grammar Exercise

Indicate the grammatical function Ⓕ and meaning Ⓔ of the word "之" in the following sentences.

1. 宣王說之

    Ⓕ _____

    Ⓔ _____

2. 好一一聽之

  Ⓕ _____

  Ⓔ _____

✎ III. Rearrangement

Rearrange the following Chinese characters in the correct word order.

1. 齊宣王 / 竽 / 人 / 吹 / 使 / ，/ 百 / 人 / 必 / 三 / 。

  _____

2. 竽 / 南郭 / 王 / 請 / 為 / 處士 / 吹 / 。

  _____

3. 宣王 / 之 / 說 / ，/ 以 / 廩食 / 百 / 數 / 人 / 。

  _____

4. 死 / 宣王 / ，/ 立 / 湣王 / ，/ 好 / 一一 / 之 / 聽 / ，/ 逃 / 處士 / 。

  _____

Ancient Fables (Part 1: C)

一. 寓言選 (上)

(丙) 守株待兔

✎ I. Text Exercise

Fill in the blanks below. Use one Chinese character for each blank.

宋人有耕_____，田中_____株，兔_____觸株，折頸_____死。

_____釋其耒_____守株，冀復得兔。兔不_____復得，_____身

_____宋國笑。

✎ II. Punctuation Exercise

Put a dot after each sentence.

宋 人 有 耕 者 田 中 有 株 兔 走 觸 株 折 頸

而 死 因 釋 其 耒 而 守 株 冀 復 得 兔 兔 不

可 復 得 而 身 為 宋 國 笑

✎ III. Translation

Translate the passage in Section (II) into English.

_____

_____

_____

_____

_____

_____

_____

_____

_____

_____

eabababababababababababababababab *1* eabababababababababababababababab

Ancient Fables (Part 1: D)

一. 寓言選 (上)
(丁) 畫蛇添足

✏ **I. Grammar Exercise**

Indicate the grammatical function Ⓕ and meaning Ⓔ of the word "其" in the following sentences.

1. 賜<u>其</u>舍人卮酒

　　Ⓕ _____

　　Ⓔ _____

2. 奪<u>其</u>卮曰

　　Ⓕ _____

　　Ⓔ _____

3. 遂飲<u>其</u>酒

　　Ⓕ _____

　　Ⓔ _____

4. 終亡其酒

Ⓔ _____

Ⓐ _____

✎ II. Rearrangement

Rearrange the following Chinese characters in the correct word order.

1. 祠 / 者 / 楚 / 有 / ， / 卮 / 其 / 舍人 / 賜 / 酒 / 。

_____

2. 謂 / 曰 / 舍人 / 相 / ： / 之 / 數人 / 不足 / 飲 / ， / 飲 有 / 一人 / 餘 / 之 / 。

_____

3. 蛇 / 請 / 地 / 畫 / 為 / ， / 成 / 酒 / 者 / 飲 / 先 / 。

_____

4. 成 / 一人 / 蛇 / 先 / ， / 且 / 之 / 引 / 酒 / 飲 / 。

_____

5. 乃 / 持 / 左手 / 卮 / ， / 畫 / 右手 / 蛇 / 曰 / ： / 足 / 為 / 吾 / 能 / 之 / 。

_____

6. 成 / 未 / ， / 一人 / 之 / 成 / 蛇 / ， / 卮 / 奪 / 其 / 曰 / 。

_____

7. 足 / 蛇 / 固 / 無 / ， / 安 / 能 / 為 / 之 / 足 / 子 / ？ / 遂 / 酒 / 飲 / 其 / 。

_____

8. 為 / 者 / 蛇 / 足 / ， / 終 / 其 / 酒 / 亡 / 。

_____

Ancient Fables (Part 2: A)

二. 寓言選(下)
(甲) 狐假虎威

✎ **I. Text Exercise (1)**

Fill in the blanks below. Use one Chinese character for each blank.

虎_____百獸而食_____，_____狐。狐曰：「子_____敢食我也！
天帝_____我長百獸，今子_____我，_____逆天帝命_____。子
_____我為不信，吾_____子先行，子_____我後，觀百獸_____見
我_____敢不走_____？」虎以為_____，故遂_____之行，獸見之
_____走，虎_____知獸畏己_____走也，以為_____狐也。

✎ **II. Text Exercise (2)**

Fill in the blanks below. Use 之, 而, or 也.

1. 助之長者，揠苗者_____。

2. 虎求百獸_____食之，得狐。

3. 數人飲＿＿＿＿不足，一人飲＿＿＿＿有餘。

4. 一人＿＿＿＿蛇成，奪其卮曰。

5. 宋人有閔其苗之不長＿＿＿＿揠之者。

6. 非徒無益，＿＿＿＿又害之。

7. 虎不知獸畏己＿＿＿＿走也，以為畏狐＿＿＿＿。

8. 兔走觸株，折頸＿＿＿＿死。

═══════════ 2 ═══════════

Ancient Fables (Part 2: B)

二. 寓言選 (下)
(乙) 刻舟求劍

✎ **I. Text Exercise (1)**

Fill in the blanks below. Use one Chinese character for each blank.

楚人有涉江＿＿＿＿，＿＿＿＿劍自舟中墜＿＿＿＿水，＿＿＿＿契其舟曰：

「＿＿＿＿吾劍＿＿＿＿＿＿＿＿從墜。」舟止。＿＿＿＿其＿＿＿＿契者入水求

＿＿＿＿，舟已行＿＿＿＿，＿＿＿＿劍不行，求劍＿＿＿＿此，不＿＿＿＿惑

＿＿＿＿？

✎ **II. Text Exercise (2)**

Fill in the blanks below. Use either 者 or 所.

1. 宋人有閔其苗之不長而揠之＿＿＿＿。

2. 是吾劍之＿＿＿＿從墜。

3. 楚有祠_____，賜其舍人卮酒。

4. 楚人有涉江_____，其劍自舟中墜於水。

5. 從其_____契者入水求之。

6. 宋人有耕_____。

<pre><code>2</code></pre>

Ancient Fables (Part 2: C)

二. 寓言選（下）
（丙）塞翁失馬

✎ I. Punctuation Exercise

Put a dot after each sentence.

近 塞 上 之 人 有 善 術 者 馬 無 故 亡 而 入 胡 人 皆

弔 之 其 父 曰 此 何 遽 不 為 福 乎 居 數 月 其 馬 將 胡

駿 馬 而 歸 人 皆 賀 之 其 父 曰 此 何 遽 不 能 為 禍 乎

家 富 良 馬 其 子 好 騎 墜 而 折 其 髀 人 皆 弔 之 其 父

曰 此 何 遽 不 為 福 乎

✎ II. Text Exercise (1)

Fill in the blanks below. Use one Chinese character for each blank.

居 一＿＿＿＿ ，＿＿＿＿ 人 大 入＿＿＿＿ ，丁 壯＿＿＿＿ 引 弦＿＿＿＿ 戰 。 近 塞

上＿＿＿＿人，死＿＿＿＿十九。此＿＿＿＿以跛之＿＿＿＿，父子＿＿＿＿

保。＿＿＿＿福之＿＿＿＿禍，禍＿＿＿＿為福，＿＿＿＿不可極，＿＿＿＿不

可測＿＿＿＿。

✏️ III. Text Exercise (2)

Fill in the blanks below. Use 其, 乎, or 矣.

1. ＿＿＿＿父曰：「此何遽不為福＿＿＿＿？」

2. 今日病＿＿＿＿，予助苗長＿＿＿＿！

3. 家富良馬，＿＿＿＿子好騎，墜而折＿＿＿＿髀，人皆弔之。

4. 天下之不助苗長者寡＿＿＿＿！

5. 子隨我後，觀百獸之見我而敢不走＿＿＿＿？

6. 為蛇足者，終亡＿＿＿＿酒。

7. 從其所契者入水求之，舟已行＿＿＿＿。

8. 宋人有閔＿＿＿＿苗之不長而揠之者。

9. ＿＿＿＿子趨而往視之，苗則槁＿＿＿＿。

10. 求劍若此，不亦惑＿＿＿＿？

Ancient Fables (Part 2: D)

二. 寓言選 (下)

(丁) 葉公好龍

✎ I. Text Exercise

Fill in the blanks below. Use one Chinese character for each blank.

葉公子高＿＿＿＿龍，鉤＿＿＿＿寫龍，＿＿＿＿ ＿＿＿＿寫龍，屋室雕文
＿＿＿＿寫龍，＿＿＿＿是天龍聞＿＿＿＿下＿＿＿＿，＿＿＿＿頭＿＿＿＿牖，
施＿＿＿＿於堂。葉公＿＿＿＿ ＿＿＿＿，棄＿＿＿＿還＿＿＿＿，失＿＿＿＿魂
＿＿＿＿，＿＿＿＿色無＿＿＿＿。是葉公＿＿＿＿好龍＿＿＿＿，好＿＿＿＿似
龍而非龍＿＿＿＿也。

✎ II. Translation

Translate the following passage into English.

孫叔敖[1] 為嬰兒[2] 之時，出遊，見兩頭蛇，殺而埋[3] 之。歸而泣。其
母問其故[4]。叔敖對曰：「聞見兩頭之蛇者死；嚮[5] 者吾見之，恐[6] 去

母而死也。」其母曰：「蛇今安[7]在？」曰：「恐他人又見，殺而埋之矣。」其母曰：「吾聞有陰德[8]者，天報[9]以福，汝不死也。」及[10]長為楚令尹[11]，未治而國人信其仁[12]也。

《新序》：兩頭蛇

註釋 (Annotations)

1. 孫叔敖　　Sūn Shū Áo　　name of a person.

2. 嬰兒　　　yīng ér　　　child.

3. 埋　　　　mái　　　　　to bury.

4. 故　　　　gù　　　　　reason.

5. 嚮　　　　xiàng　　　　just now.

6. 恐　　　　kǒng　　　　to be afraid of.

7. 安　　　　ān　　　　　where?

8. 陰德　　　yīn dé　　　hidden virtue of goodness.

9. 報　　　　bào　　　　　to repay.

10. 及　　　　jí　　　　　by the time when.

11. 令尹　　　lìng yǐn　　　chief minister.

12. 仁　　　　rén　　　　　benevolence.

Selections from the *Lunyu* (Part 1)

三.《論語》選（上）

✎ I. Text Exercise (1)

Fill in the blanks below. Use one Chinese character for each blank.

1. 子曰：「學而＿＿＿習之，＿＿＿＿亦＿＿＿＿乎？」

2. 有朋＿＿＿＿遠＿＿＿＿來，不亦＿＿＿＿乎？＿＿＿＿不＿＿＿＿而不
   ＿＿＿＿，不＿＿＿＿君子＿＿＿＿？

3. 曾子曰：「＿＿＿＿日＿＿＿＿省＿＿＿＿身：為人＿＿＿＿而不＿＿＿＿
   乎？＿＿＿＿朋友＿＿＿＿而不＿＿＿＿乎？＿＿＿＿不習＿＿＿＿？」

4. 子貢曰：「孔文子，＿＿＿＿以＿＿＿＿之文＿＿＿＿？」子曰：「＿＿＿＿
   而好學，不＿＿＿＿下問，＿＿＿＿以＿＿＿＿之文也。」

5. 子曰：「若＿＿＿與仁，則＿＿＿豈＿＿＿？＿＿＿為之不
　　＿＿＿，誨人不＿＿＿，則可謂云＿＿＿已＿＿＿！」公西華曰：
　　「正＿＿＿弟子不＿＿＿學＿＿＿。」

✎ II. Text Exercise (2)

Fill in the blanks below. Use 而, 則, or 之.

1. 其子趨＿＿＿往視＿＿＿，苗＿＿＿槁矣。

2. 人不知＿＿＿不慍，不亦君子乎？

3. 抑為之不厭，誨人不倦，＿＿＿可謂云爾已矣！

4. 馬無故亡＿＿＿入胡，人皆弔＿＿＿。

5. 學＿＿＿時習＿＿＿，不亦說乎？

6. 為人謀＿＿＿不忠乎？

7. 敏＿＿＿好學，不恥下問。

8. 兔走觸株，折頸＿＿＿死。

9. 若聖與仁，＿＿＿吾豈敢？

10. 虎不知獸畏己＿＿＿走也，以為畏狐也。

╼╼╼╼╼╼╼╼╼╼╼╼╼╼╼╼╼╼╼ *4* ╼╼╼╼╼╼╼╼╼╼╼╼╼╼╼╼╼╼╼

Selections from the *Lunyu* (Part 2)

四.《論語》選(中)

✎ I. Text Exercise

Fill in the blanks below. Use one Chinese character for each blank.

1. 顏淵季路_____，子曰：「_____各言_____志？」

2. 子路_____：「_____車馬衣_____ _____與朋友_____，_____ 之_____無憾。」

3. 顏淵曰：「無_____善，_____施_____。」

4. 子路曰：「願_____子之_____。」子曰：「_____者安之，朋友 _____之，少_____ _____之。」

5. 子路問：「_____斯行_____？」子曰：「有_____兄_____，如之 _____其聞_____行_____？」

6. 冉有＿＿＿＿＿：「聞＿＿＿＿＿行諸？」子曰：「＿＿＿＿＿斯行＿＿＿＿＿。」

7. 公西華曰：「由＿＿＿＿＿問，『聞斯＿＿＿＿＿諸』；子曰：『有父＿＿＿＿＿
   在。』」

8. 求＿＿＿＿＿問：『聞斯行＿＿＿＿＿？』；子曰：『聞斯行＿＿＿＿＿。』

9. 赤也＿＿＿＿＿，＿＿＿＿＿問。

10. 子曰：「求也＿＿＿＿＿，＿＿＿＿＿進＿＿＿＿＿。由也＿＿＿＿＿人，故退
    ＿＿＿＿＿。」

5

Selections from the *Lunyu* (Part 3)

五.《論語》選（下）

I. Text Exercise

Fill in the blanks below. Use one Chinese character for each blank.

1. 子______武城，______弦歌之______。夫子______爾而______。

2. 「割雞______用牛______？」

3. 『君子學______則______人，______人學道______易使______。』

4. 叔孫武叔______大夫於______曰：「子貢賢______仲______。」

5. 夫子之______，不______宜乎？

II. Punctuation Exercise

Put a dot after each sentence.

1. 子 游 對 曰 昔 者 偃 也 聞 諸 夫 子 曰 君 子 學 道

則 愛 人 小 人 學 道 則 易 使 也 子 曰 二 三 子 偃

之 言 是 也 前 言 戲 之 耳

2. 子 貢 曰 譬 之 宮 牆 賜 之 牆 也 及 肩 闚 見 室 家

之 好 夫 子 之 牆 數 仞 不 得 其 門 而 入 不 見 宗

廟 之 美 百 官 之 富 得 其 門 者 或 寡 矣

✏ III. Review Exercise

Fill in the blanks below with the following grammatical particles.
(1) Sentence-end particles: 也, 矣, 乎, 耳; (2) Conjunctions: 而, 則; (3) Coverbs: 於, 以, 為, 自, 與; (4) Others: 者, 諸, 其.

1. 小人學道_____易使也。

2. 鉤_____寫龍，鑿_____寫龍，屋室雕文_____寫龍。

3. _____朋友交而不信乎？

4. 請畫地_____蛇。

5. 老_____安之，朋友信之，少_____懷之。

6. _____劍_____舟中墜於水。

7. 君子學道_____愛人。

8. 子_____我為不信，吾_____子先行。

9. 夫子_____云，不亦宜_____？

10. 吾能_____之足。

11. 如之何其聞斯行_____？

12. 子貢賢_____仲尼。

13. 子服景伯_____告子貢。

14. 子之武城，聞弦歌_____聲。

15. 抑為_____不厭，誨人不倦，則可謂云爾已_____！

16. 為蛇足者，終亡_____酒。

17. 故福_____為禍，禍_____為福，化不可極，深不可測_____。

18. 願車馬衣輕裘_____朋友共，敝之_____無憾。

19. 求劍若此，不亦惑_____？

20. 二三子，偃_____言是也，前言戲之_____。

ereereereereereereereereereereer **6** ereereereereereereereereereereereer

Selection from the *Mengzi* (Part 1)

六.《孟子・梁惠王上》(節)

 I. Text Exercise

Fill in the blanks below. Use one Chinese character for each blank.

1. 孟子＿＿＿＿梁惠王。王曰：「＿＿＿＿＿！不＿＿＿＿千里＿＿＿＿來，
   ＿＿＿＿將有＿＿＿＿利吾國＿＿＿＿？」

2. 孟子＿＿＿＿曰：「王＿＿＿＿必曰＿＿＿＿？＿＿＿＿有仁＿＿＿＿而已
   ＿＿＿＿。」

3. 王＿＿＿＿：「何以＿＿＿＿吾＿＿＿＿？」＿＿＿＿夫曰：「＿＿＿＿以利吾
   ＿＿＿＿？」士＿＿＿＿人曰：「何＿＿＿＿利吾＿＿＿＿？」

4. 上下＿＿＿＿征＿＿＿＿而國＿＿＿＿矣。

5. ＿＿＿＿為＿＿＿＿義而先＿＿＿＿，不＿＿＿＿不＿＿＿＿。

✎ II. Punctuation Exercise

Put a dot after each sentence.

1. 萬 乘 之 國 弒 其 君 者 必 千 乘 之 家 千 乘 之 家 弒 其 君 者 必 百 乘 之 家 萬 取 千 焉 千 取 百 焉 不 為 不 多 矣

2. 未 有 仁 而 遺 其 親 者 也 未 有 義 而 後 其 君 者 也 王 亦 曰 仁 義 而 已 矣 何 必 曰 利

━━━━━━━━━━━━━━━━━━━━ 7 ━━━━━━━━━━━━━━━━━━━━

Selection from the *Mengzi* (Part 2)

七.《孟子·梁惠王下》(節)

✎ I. Text Exercise

Fill in the blanks below. Use one Chinese character for each blank.

1. 或謂寡人_____取，或_____寡人取_____。

2. _____萬乘之國_____萬乘之國，五_____而_____之，人力不_____於此。

3. 取之_____燕_____悦，_____取之。古_____人_____行之_____，武王是_____。

4. 以_____乘之國_____萬乘之國，_____食_____漿以_____王師，豈有他_____？_____水火也。

5. 如水_____深，_____火益熱，亦_____而已_____。

✎ II. Grammar Exercise

Indicate the grammatical function Ⓕ and meaning Ⓔ of the word "於" in the following sentences.

1. 移其民於河東。(《孟子 · 梁惠王上》)

   Ⓕ _____

   Ⓔ _____

2. 叔孫武叔語大夫於朝曰。(《論語 · 子張》)

   Ⓕ _____

   Ⓔ _____

3. 苛政猛於虎也。(《禮記 · 檀弓下》)

   Ⓕ _____

   Ⓔ _____

4. 其劍自舟中墜於水。(寓言：刻舟求劍)

   Ⓕ _____

   Ⓔ _____

5. 寡人之於國也。(《孟子 · 梁惠王上》)

   Ⓕ _____

   Ⓔ _____

6. 人力不至於此。(《孟子 · 梁惠王下》)

   Ⓕ _____

   Ⓔ _____

7. 窺頭於牖，施尾於堂。(寓言：葉公好龍)

　　Ⓕ _____

　　Ⓔ _____

8. 子貢賢於仲尼。(《論語‧子張》)

　　Ⓕ _____

　　Ⓔ _____

9. 有楚大夫於此。(《孟子‧滕文公下》)

　　Ⓕ _____

　　Ⓔ _____

10.子謂薛居州善士也，使之居於王所。在於王所者，長幼卑尊皆薛
　　居州也。(《孟子‧滕文公下》)

　　Ⓕ _____

　　Ⓔ _____

〰〰〰〰〰〰〰〰〰〰〰〰 *8* 〰〰〰〰〰〰〰〰〰〰〰〰〰

Selection from the *Mengzi*

八.《孟子‧滕文公下》(節)

📝 I. Reading Comprehension

Read the following passage.

《孟子‧梁惠王上》(節)

梁惠王曰:「寡人之於國也,盡心焉耳矣。河內凶,[1]則移其民於河東,[2]移其粟於河內;[3]河東凶,亦然。察鄰國之政,[4]無如寡人之用心者,鄰國之民不加少,寡人之民不加多,[5]何也?」

孟子對曰:「王好戰,請以戰喻,[6]填然鼓之,[7]兵刃既接,[8]棄甲曳兵而走,[9]或百步而後止,或五十步而後止,以五十步笑百步,則何如?」曰:「不可,直不百步耳,[10]是亦走也。」

註 釋 (Annotations)

1. 河內　Hé nèi　　the area within the bend of the (Yellow) River.

   凶　　xiōng　　unlucky; here, it means specifically "[a year] of poor harvest".

2. 河東　Hé dōng　the area to the east of the (Yellow) River.

3. 粟　　sù　　　millet.

4. 察　　chá　　to observe.

5. 加　　jiā　　to change (in terms of quantity).

6. 喻　　yù　　to explain or illustrate (with an example or metaphor).

7. 填然　tián rán　with a bang (填 is an onomatopoeia for the sound of the drum, compare with "tap-tap".)

   鼓　　gǔ　　(used as a verb) to give the signal to advance (in a military attack).

8. 兵　　bīng　weapons.

   刃　　rèn　　the cutting edge of a sharp weapon.

   既　　jì　　already.

   接　　jiē　　to come into contact; to be connected.

9. 棄　　qì　　to throw down; to drop.

   曳　　yè　　to drag (along the ground).

10. 直　　zhí　only, merely.

1. Grammar Exercise

Indicate the grammatical function Ⓕ and meaning Ⓔ of the word "之" in the following sentences. Note that "之" can be used as a pronoun, a possessive marker, or a marker for the subordination of a simple sentence.

1. 無如寡人之用心者

   Ⓕ _____

   Ⓔ _____

2. 寡人之於國也

    Ⓕ _____

    Ⓔ _____

3. 鄰國之民不加少

    Ⓕ _____

    Ⓔ _____

4. 寡人之民不加多

    Ⓕ _____

    Ⓔ _____

5. 填然鼓之

    Ⓕ _____

    Ⓔ _____

2. Translation

Translate the passage into English.

_____

_____

_____

_____

_____

9

Selections from the *Liji*

九.《禮記》選

✏ **I. Punctuation Exercise**

Put a dot after each sentence.

1. 曾 子 以 斯 言 告 於 子 游 子 游 曰 甚 哉 有 子
   之 言 似 夫 子 也 昔 者 夫 子 居 於 宋 見 桓 司
   馬 自 為 石 槨 三 年 而 不 成 夫 子 曰 若 是 其
   靡 也 死 不 如 速 朽 之 愈 也

2. 孔 子 過 泰 山 側 有 婦 人 哭 於 墓 者 而 哀 夫
   子 式 而 聽 之 使 子 路 問 之 曰 子 之 哭 也 壹
   似 重 有 憂 者 而 曰 然

✎ II. Crossword Puzzle

Read the text again and do the following crossword.

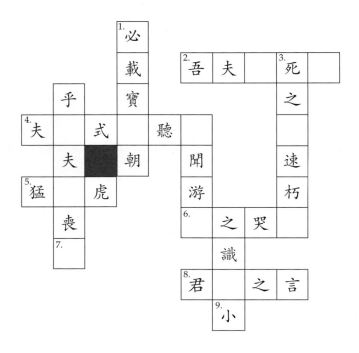

Vertical:

1. 必載寶＿＿朝

3. 死之＿＿速朽＿＿

6. ＿＿游聞＿＿ (inverted)

7. ＿＿喪＿＿夫＿＿乎 (inverted)

9. 小＿＿識之 (inverted)

Horizontal:

2. 吾夫＿＿死＿＿

4. 夫＿＿式＿＿聽＿＿

5. 猛＿＿虎

6. ＿＿之哭＿＿

8. 君＿＿之言

10

Selection from the *Laozi*

十．《老子》選

✏ **I. Text Exercise**

Fill in the blanks below. Use one Chinese character for each blank.

1. ＿＿＿ ＿＿＿廢，有仁義。＿＿＿ ＿＿＿出，＿＿＿大偽。

   ＿＿＿ ＿＿＿不和，有孝慈。＿＿＿ ＿＿＿昏亂，有忠臣。

2. 天下＿＿＿柔弱＿＿＿水，＿＿＿攻堅強＿＿＿莫之能＿＿＿，

   ＿＿＿其無以易＿＿＿。

3. 雖有＿＿＿ ＿＿＿，＿＿＿ ＿＿＿乘之；雖有＿＿＿ ＿＿＿，無

   所陳之；使人＿＿＿結＿＿＿而用之。

✎ II. Grammar Exercise

Analyze the causative and putative usages.

1. What is the special aspect of the sentence 小國寡民？ Please find more examples from the previous lessons.

   _____

   _____

   _____

2. What is the special aspect of the sentence 甘其食，美其服，安其居，樂其俗？ Please find more examples from the previous lessons.

   _____

   _____

   _____

✎ III. Translation

Translate the following passage into English.

　　道可道，非常道。[1] 名可名，非常名。[2] 無名，天地之始。[3] 有名，萬物之母。[4] 故常無欲，以觀其妙。[5] 常有欲，以觀其徼。[6] 兩者同出而異名。同謂主玄，玄之又玄。[7] 眾妙之門。[8]

　　　　　　　　　　　　　　　　《老子》：第一章

註 釋 (Annotations)

1. 可   kě   may.

    常   cháng   everlasting; constant.

2. 名   míng   name (of a thing).

3. 始   shǐ   origin.

4. 萬物   wàn wù   all things on earth.

    母   mǔ   the beginning.

5. 觀   guān   to observe.

    妙   miào   secret; mystery.

6. 徼   jiào   boundaries; signs.

7. 玄   xuán   mysterious and metaphysical.

8. 眾   zhòng   all.

    門   mén   the gateway.

⌇⌇⌇⌇⌇⌇⌇⌇⌇⌇⌇⌇⌇⌇⌇⌇⌇⌇⌇⌇⌇⌇ *11* ⌇⌇⌇⌇⌇⌇⌇⌇⌇⌇⌇⌇⌇⌇⌇⌇⌇⌇⌇⌇⌇⌇⌇

Selection from the *Mozi*

十一.《墨子・公輸》：墨子說公輸盤

✎ I. Matching

Which follows which? Read the text again and match up the sentences. Write the letters on the lines.

1. 荊國有餘於地，_____。　　　A. 行十日十夜而至於郢

2. 子墨子聞之，_____。　　　　B. 不可謂智

3. 爭而不得，_____。　　　　　C. 造雲梯之械

4. 北方有侮臣 (者)，_____。　　D. 不可謂仁

5. 義不殺少而殺眾，_____。　　E. 起於齊

6. 殺所不足而爭所有餘，_____。F. 不可謂知類

7. 宋無罪而攻之，_____。　　　G. 不可謂忠

8. 知而不爭，_____。　　　　　H. 而不足於民

9. 起於齊，_____。　　　　　　I. 不可謂強

10. 公輸盤為楚_____。　　　　　J. 願藉子殺之

✎ II. Grammar Exercise

Fill in the blanks below with the particles 於, 從, 之, 焉, 而, 以, 為, 不, 無, 何, or 所.

1. 吾＿＿＿＿北方，聞子＿＿＿＿梯，將＿＿＿＿攻宋。

2. 宋＿＿＿＿罪＿＿＿＿攻之。

3. 夫子＿＿＿＿命＿＿＿＿為？

4. 吾義固＿＿＿＿殺人。

5. 行十日十夜＿＿＿＿至＿＿＿＿郢。

6. 殺＿＿＿＿不足＿＿＿＿爭所有餘，＿＿＿＿可謂智。

7. 宋何罪＿＿＿＿有？

8. 子墨子聞＿＿＿＿，起＿＿＿＿齊。

12

Selection from the *Zhuangzi* (No. 1)

十二.《莊子・秋水》(節)

✎ **I. Text Exercise**

Fill in the blanks below. Use one Chinese character for each blank.

　　秋水＿＿＿至，百川灌＿＿＿。涇流＿＿＿大，兩涘＿＿＿崖之間，＿＿＿辯牛馬。＿＿＿ ＿＿＿ ＿＿＿河伯欣然自喜，＿＿＿天下之美為盡在己。順流＿＿＿東行，至＿＿＿北海；東面＿＿＿視，＿＿＿見水端。

　　於是焉河伯＿＿＿旋＿＿＿面目，望洋＿＿＿若而歎曰：「＿＿＿ ＿＿＿有之曰：『聞道百，＿＿＿為莫己若』者，我之謂＿＿＿。＿＿＿我嘗聞＿＿＿仲尼之聞，而＿＿＿伯夷之義者，始吾＿＿＿信，今我睹子之難窮＿＿＿，吾＿＿＿至於子之門，＿＿＿殆矣，吾長見笑＿＿＿大方＿＿＿家。」

✎ II. Grammar Exercise

Fill in the blanks with the negative particles 不, 無, 非, 勿, 弗, 未, or 莫.

1. 宋人有閔其苗之＿＿＿＿＿長而揠之者。

2. 始吾＿＿＿＿＿信，今我睹子之難窮也，吾＿＿＿＿＿至於子之門，則殆矣。

3. 取之而燕民＿＿＿＿＿悅，則＿＿＿＿＿取。

4. 雖有舟輿，＿＿＿＿＿所乘之；雖有甲兵，＿＿＿＿＿所陳之。

5. 弱之勝強，柔之勝剛，天下＿＿＿＿＿不知，＿＿＿＿＿能行。

6. ＿＿＿＿＿有仁而遺其親者也，＿＿＿＿＿有義而後其君者也。

13

Selection from the *Zhuangzi* (No. 2)

十三.《莊子・徐無鬼》：運斤成風

✏ I. Grammar Exercise

Indicate the grammatical function Ⓕ and meaning Ⓔ of the word "之" in the following sentences.

1. 莊子送葬，過惠子之墓。

   Ⓕ _____

   Ⓔ _____

2. 臣則嘗能斲之。

   Ⓕ _____

   Ⓔ _____

3. 自夫子之死也。

   Ⓕ _____

   Ⓔ _____

4. 吾無與言之矣！

F _____

E _____

5. 子之哭也，壹似重有憂者？

F _____

E _____

6. 取之而燕民悦，則取之。

F _____

E _____

7. 甚哉，有子之言似夫子也！

F _____

E _____

8. 子之武城，聞弦歌之聲。

F _____

E _____

9. 子欲子之王之善與？

F _____

E _____

✎ II. Translation

Translate the following passage into English.

魚之樂

　　莊子與惠子遊於濠梁之上。[1] 莊子曰：「儵魚出游從容，[2] 是魚之樂也。」惠子曰：「子非魚，安知魚之樂？」莊子曰：「子非我，安知我之不知魚之樂？」惠子曰：「我非子，固不知子矣；子固非魚也，子之不知魚之樂全矣。」莊子曰：「請循其本。[3]子曰：『汝安知魚樂』云者，既已知吾知之而問我。[4] 我知之濠上也。」

《莊子‧秋水》

註 釋 (Annotations)

1.	惠子	Hùi Zǐ	name of a person. A good friend of 莊子.
	濠梁	Háo liáng	the bridge of the Hao River. 梁 is a bridge.
2.	儵魚	chóu yú	a small white fish.
	從容	cōng róng	leisurely.
3.	循	xún	to follow.
4.	既已	jì yǐ	already.

_____

_____

_____

_____

_____

_____

14

Selection from the *Xunzi*

十四.《荀子・勸學》(節)

✎ **I. Text Exercise**

Fill in the blanks below. Use one Chinese character for each blank.

1. 君子曰：學不可以＿＿＿。青，＿＿＿之＿＿＿藍，而＿＿＿於藍；＿＿＿，水為之，而＿＿＿於水。

2. 故＿＿＿受繩＿＿＿直，金就＿＿＿則利，君子＿＿＿＿＿＿而日＿＿＿省＿＿＿己，＿＿＿知明＿＿＿行無＿＿＿矣。

3. 故不登＿＿＿＿＿＿，不知天之＿＿＿也；不＿＿＿深＿＿＿，不知＿＿＿之厚也；不聞＿＿＿＿＿＿之遺言，＿＿＿知＿＿＿問之＿＿＿也。

4. 故不積＿＿＿步，＿＿＿以＿＿＿千里；不＿＿＿小＿＿＿，無以＿＿＿江＿＿＿。

5. 鍥而＿＿＿之，＿＿＿木不＿＿＿；＿＿＿而＿＿＿舍，金＿＿＿

可＿＿＿。

6. 是＿＿＿＿無冥＿＿＿之＿＿＿者，＿＿＿昭昭之＿＿＿；無＿＿＿

惛＿＿＿事＿＿＿，無＿＿＿赫之＿＿＿。

II. Grammar Exercise

Indicate the grammatical function Ⓕ and meaning Ⓔ of the word "於" in the following sentences.

1. 青，取之<u>於</u>藍，而青<u>於</u>藍；冰，水為之，而寒<u>於</u>水。

Ⓕ ＿＿＿＿＿＿＿＿＿＿＿＿＿＿＿＿＿＿＿＿＿＿＿＿＿＿＿

Ⓔ ＿＿＿＿＿＿＿＿＿＿＿＿＿＿＿＿＿＿＿＿＿＿＿＿＿＿＿

2. 吾非至<u>於</u>子之門，則殆矣，吾長見笑<u>於</u>大方之家。

Ⓕ ＿＿＿＿＿＿＿＿＿＿＿＿＿＿＿＿＿＿＿＿＿＿＿＿＿＿＿

Ⓔ ＿＿＿＿＿＿＿＿＿＿＿＿＿＿＿＿＿＿＿＿＿＿＿＿＿＿＿

3. 天下莫柔弱<u>於</u>水。

Ⓕ ＿＿＿＿＿＿＿＿＿＿＿＿＿＿＿＿＿＿＿＿＿＿＿＿＿＿＿

Ⓔ ＿＿＿＿＿＿＿＿＿＿＿＿＿＿＿＿＿＿＿＿＿＿＿＿＿＿＿

CRCRCRCRCRCRCRCRCRCRCRCRCRCRCRCR *15* CRCRCRCRCRCRCRCRCRCRCRCRCRCRCRCRCR

Selection from the *Han Feizi*

十五.《韓非子 · 說林上》：巧詐不如拙誠

✎ I. Rearrangement

Rearrange the following Chinese characters in the correct word order.

1. 中山 / 其 / 君 / 烹 / 之 / 子 / 而 / 之 / 羹 / 遺 / 。

---

2. 之 / 子 / 食 / 其 / 而 / ， / 食 / 誰 / 不 / 且 / ？

---

3. 功 / 文 / 賞 / 疑 / 其 / 而 / 其 / 心 / 侯 / 。

---

4. 麑 / 夫 / 忍 / 不 / ， / 乎 / 又 / 忍 / 吾 / 且 / 子 / ？

---

5. 不 / 誠 / 巧 / 拙 / 如 / 詐 / 。

---

6. 樂羊 / 功 / 疑 / 以 / 見 / 有 / ， / 秦西巴 / 信 / 有 / 益 / 以 / 罪 / 。

_____

✎ II. Grammar Exercise

The coverb "與" can be a verb and a preposition. Indicate the grammatical function Ⓕ and meaning Ⓔ of it in the following sentences.

1. 與朋友交而不信乎？

   Ⓕ _____

   Ⓔ _____

2. 若聖與仁，則吾豈敢？

   Ⓕ _____

   Ⓔ _____

3. 余弗忍而與其母。

   Ⓕ _____

   Ⓔ _____

4. 願車馬衣輕裘與朋友共。

   Ⓕ _____

   Ⓔ _____

5. 吾無與言之矣！

   Ⓕ _____

   Ⓔ _____

Selection from the *Zuozhuan* (No. 1)

十六.《左傳‧莊公十年》：曹劌論戰

✎ I. Matching

Which follows which? Read the text again and match up the sentences. Write the letters on the blanks.

1. 肉食者謀之，___B___   A. 神弗福也。

2. 小信未孚，___A___   B. 又何間焉？

3. 夫戰，___E___   C. 必以情。

4. 吾視其轍亂，望其旗靡，___I___   D. 登軾而望之。

5. 夫大國，___F___   E. 勇氣也。

6. 忠之屬也，___H___   F. 難測也。

7. 犧牲玉帛，弗敢加也，___J___   G. 再而衰，三而竭。

8. 一鼓作氣，___G___   H. 可以一戰。

9. 下視其轍，___D___   I. 故逐之。

10. 小大之獄，雖不能察，___C___   J. 必以信。

✎ II. Translation

Translate the following sentences.

1. 衣食所安，弗敢專也，必以分人。

_____

2. 小大之獄，雖不能察，必以情。

_____

3. 小信未孚，神弗福也。

_____

4. 齊師敗績，公將馳之，劌曰：「未可。」

_____

5. 下視其轍，登軾而望之。

_____

ececececececececececececececececececececec *17* ececececececececececececececececececececec

Selection from the *Zuozhuan* (No. 2)

十七.《左傳・僖公四年》：齊桓公伐楚

✎ **I. Text Exercise**

Fill in the blanks below. Use one Chinese character for each blank.

1. 四年春，齊侯 <u>以</u> 諸侯之師侵蔡。蔡潰，<u>遂</u> 伐楚。

2. 爾 <u>貢</u> 包茅不入，王祭不 <u>共</u> ，<u>無</u> 以縮酒，寡人是 <u>徵</u> 。

3. 師進，次 <u>于</u> 陘。

4. 齊侯 <u>陳</u> 諸侯 <u>之</u> 師，<u>與</u> 屈完乘 <u>而</u> 觀之。

5. 君 <u>若</u> 以德 <u>綏</u> 諸侯，誰敢不 <u>服</u> 。

6. 君若以力楚國方城 <u>以</u> 為城，漢水 <u>以</u> 為池，<u>雖</u> 眾，<u>無</u> <u>所</u> 用之！

✎ II. Translation

Write down the meaning of the underlined words and then translate the sentences.

1. 昭王<u>之</u>不復，君<u>其</u>問諸水濱！

   之：_____

   其：_____

   整句翻譯：_____

   _____

   _____

2. 夏，楚子<u>使</u>屈完<u>如</u>師。

   使：_____

   如：_____

   整句翻譯：_____

   _____

   _____

3. <u>師</u>退，<u>次</u>于召陵。

   師：_____

   次：_____

   整句翻譯：_____

   _____

   _____

4. <u>以</u>此眾戰，誰能<u>禦</u>之？

以：_____

禦：_____

整句翻譯：_____

_____

_____

✎ III. Grammar Exercise and Translation

First, indicate the grammatical function Ⓕ and meaning Ⓔ of the word "是" in the following sentences. Then translate Ⓣ the sentences into English.

1. 唯<u>是</u>風馬牛不相及也

Ⓕ _____

Ⓔ _____

Ⓣ _____

2. 寡人<u>是</u>徵

Ⓕ _____

Ⓔ _____

Ⓣ _____

3. 寡人<u>是</u>問

Ⓕ _____

Ⓔ _____

Ⓣ _____

4. 豈不穀<u>是</u>為

    Ⓕ _____

    Ⓔ _____

    Ⓣ _____

5. 先君之好<u>是</u>繼

    Ⓕ _____

    Ⓔ _____

    Ⓣ _____

‮⁊⁊⁊⁊⁊⁊⁊⁊⁊⁊⁊⁊⁊⁊⁊⁊‬ *18* ‮⁊⁊⁊⁊⁊⁊⁊⁊⁊⁊⁊⁊⁊⁊⁊⁊‬

Selection from the *Zuozhuan* (No. 3)

十八.《左傳·襄公三十一年》：子產論治

✎ **I. Text Exercise**

Fill in the blanks below. Use one Chinese character for each blank.

1. 今吾子愛人 <u>則</u> 以政， <u>猶</u> 未能操刀 <u>而</u> <u>使</u> 割也， <u>其</u> 傷 <u>實</u> 多。

2. 子 <u>之</u> 愛人，傷之而 <u>已</u> 。

3. 譬 <u>如</u> 田獵， <u>射</u> 御貫 <u>則</u> 能獲 <u>禽</u> ， <u>若</u> 未嘗 <u>登</u> 車射 <u>御</u> ，則敗 <u>績</u> 厭覆 <u>是</u> 懼， <u>何</u> 暇思獲？

4. 子皮曰：「善 <u>哉</u> ！虎不 <u>敏</u> ，吾 <u>聞</u> 君子務知 <u>大</u> 者遠 <u>者</u> ，小人 <u>務</u> 知小者 <u>近</u> 者。我小人 <u>也</u> 。」

✐ II. Translation

Translate the following sentences into English.

1. 子於鄭國，棟也。

_____

2. 大官大邑，身之所庇也。

_____

3. 其為美錦不亦多乎？

_____

4. 射御貫則能獲禽。

_____

5. 厭覆是懼。

_____

19

Selection from the *Guoyu*

十九.《國語·越語上》：句踐治越

✎ I. Text Exercise

Fill in the blanks below. Use one Chinese character for each blank.

1. 句踐_____地，南至_____句無，北至_____禦兒。

2. 將_____者_____告，公_____醫_____之。

3. _____達士，_____其居，_____其服，_____其食，_____摩
   _____之於_____。四方_____士來_____，必_____禮之。

4. 十年不收_____國，民_____有三年之_____。

5. _____孤子、_____婦、_____疹、貧病_____，納_____其子。

✎ II. Translation

Write down the meaning of the underlined words and then translate the sentences.

1. 生女子，二壺酒，一<u>豚</u>。生三人，公<u>與</u>之<u>母</u>；生二人，公<u>與</u>之
   <u>餼</u>。

   豚：＿＿＿＿＿＿＿＿＿＿＿＿＿＿＿＿＿＿＿＿＿＿＿＿

   與：＿＿＿＿＿＿＿＿＿＿＿＿＿＿＿＿＿＿＿＿＿＿＿＿

   母：＿＿＿＿＿＿＿＿＿＿＿＿＿＿＿＿＿＿＿＿＿＿＿＿

   餼：＿＿＿＿＿＿＿＿＿＿＿＿＿＿＿＿＿＿＿＿＿＿＿＿

   整句翻譯：＿＿＿＿＿＿＿＿＿＿＿＿＿＿＿＿＿＿＿＿＿

   ＿＿＿＿＿＿＿＿＿＿＿＿＿＿＿＿＿＿＿＿＿＿＿＿＿＿＿

   ＿＿＿＿＿＿＿＿＿＿＿＿＿＿＿＿＿＿＿＿＿＿＿＿＿＿＿

2. <u>當室者</u>死，三年<u>釋</u>其政；<u>支子</u>死，三月釋其政。

   當室者：＿＿＿＿＿＿＿＿＿＿＿＿＿＿＿＿＿＿＿＿＿＿

   釋：＿＿＿＿＿＿＿＿＿＿＿＿＿＿＿＿＿＿＿＿＿＿＿＿

   支子：＿＿＿＿＿＿＿＿＿＿＿＿＿＿＿＿＿＿＿＿＿＿＿

   整句翻譯：＿＿＿＿＿＿＿＿＿＿＿＿＿＿＿＿＿＿＿＿＿

   ＿＿＿＿＿＿＿＿＿＿＿＿＿＿＿＿＿＿＿＿＿＿＿＿＿＿＿

3. 國之<u>孺子</u>之遊者，無不<u>餔</u>也，無不<u>歠</u>也。

   孺子：＿＿＿＿＿＿＿＿＿＿＿＿＿＿＿＿＿＿＿＿＿＿＿

   餔：＿＿＿＿＿＿＿＿＿＿＿＿＿＿＿＿＿＿＿＿＿＿＿＿

歡：_____

整句翻譯：_____

_____

_____

✎ III. Grammar Exercise

Fill in the blanks below with the negative particles 不, 無, or 非.

1. 女子十七_____嫁，其父母有罪；丈夫二十_____娶，其父母有

   罪。

2. 子路曰：「願車馬衣輕裘與朋友共，敝之而_____憾。」顏淵曰：

   「_____伐善，_____施勞。」

3. _____其身之所種則不食，_____其夫人之所織則不衣。

4. 一齊人傅之，眾楚人咻之，雖日撻而求其齊也，_____可得矣。

5. 國之孺子之遊者，_____不餔也，_____不歡也，必問其名。

6. 是葉公_____好龍也，好夫似龍而_____龍者也。

7. 天下之_____助苗長者寡矣！以為_____益而舍之者，_____耘

   苗者也；助之長者，揠苗者也；_____徒無益，而又害之。

20

Selection from the *Zhanguo ce* (No. 1)

二十.《戰國策·齊策一》：靖郭君將城薛

✏ **I. Text Exercise**

Fill in the blanks below. Use one Chinese character for each blank.

1. 靖郭君_____城薛，客多_____諫。靖郭君_____謁者，无
   _____客通。

2. 齊人_____請_____曰：「臣_____三言而已_____！」

3. 客趨_____進曰：「海大魚。」_____反走。

4. 君曰：「客，有_____此。」客曰：「_____臣不敢_____死_____
   戲。」

5. 君_____聞大魚_____？網不能_____，鉤不能_____，蕩_____
   失水，_____螻蟻得意_____。

6. 今_____齊_____君之水_____。君長_____齊，_____以薛
_____？

✏️ II. Grammar Exercise

Fill in the blanks below with particles 乃, 夫, 也, 之, 而, or 者.

1. 「_____齊，雖隆薛_____城到於天，猶_____無益_____。」君
曰：「善。」_____輟城薛。

2. 先生所為文市義_____，_____今日見_____。

3. 劌曰：「肉食_____鄙，未能遠謀。」_____入見。

4. _____戰，勇氣_____。一鼓作氣，再_____衰，三_____竭。
彼竭我盈，故克_____。

21

Selection from the *Zhanguo ce* (No. 2)

二十一.《戰國策 · 齊策四》：馮諼客孟嘗君

✎ **I. Text Exercise**

Fill in the blanks below. Use one Chinese character for each blank.

1. 齊人有馮諼_____，貧_____不能自_____。

2. 左右_____君賤之_____，食_____草具。

3. 居有_____，倚柱彈_____劍，歌曰：「長鋏歸來_____，食_____魚！」左右_____告。

4. 孟嘗君_____之，曰：「此誰_____？」左右曰：「_____歌_____長鋏歸來_____也。」

5. 君家_____寡有者以義_____！

6. 孟嘗君曰：「＿＿＿義奈＿＿＿？」曰：「今君有＿＿＿ ＿＿＿之
  薛，不＿＿＿愛子＿＿＿民，＿＿＿而＿＿＿利＿＿＿。臣＿＿＿
  矯君命，以責＿＿＿諸民，＿＿＿燒其券，民＿＿＿萬歲。
  ＿＿＿臣所＿＿＿為君市義＿＿＿。」孟嘗君＿＿＿說，曰：
  「＿＿＿，先生休＿＿＿！」

✏️ II. Translation

Write down the meaning of the underlined words and then translate the sentences.

1. 使人屬孟嘗君，願寄食門下。

  使： ＿＿＿＿＿＿＿＿＿＿＿＿＿＿＿＿＿＿＿＿＿＿＿＿＿＿

  屬： ＿＿＿＿＿＿＿＿＿＿＿＿＿＿＿＿＿＿＿＿＿＿＿＿＿＿

  整句翻譯： ＿＿＿＿＿＿＿＿＿＿＿＿＿＿＿＿＿＿＿＿＿＿

  ＿＿＿＿＿＿＿＿＿＿＿＿＿＿＿＿＿＿＿＿＿＿＿＿＿＿＿＿

  ＿＿＿＿＿＿＿＿＿＿＿＿＿＿＿＿＿＿＿＿＿＿＿＿＿＿＿＿

2. 「客何好？」曰：「客無好也。」

  好： ＿＿＿＿＿＿＿＿＿＿＿＿＿＿＿＿＿＿＿＿＿＿＿＿＿＿

  整句翻譯： ＿＿＿＿＿＿＿＿＿＿＿＿＿＿＿＿＿＿＿＿＿＿

  ＿＿＿＿＿＿＿＿＿＿＿＿＿＿＿＿＿＿＿＿＿＿＿＿＿＿＿＿

  ＿＿＿＿＿＿＿＿＿＿＿＿＿＿＿＿＿＿＿＿＿＿＿＿＿＿＿＿

3. 於是乘其<u>車</u>，<u>揭</u>其劍，<u>過</u>其友曰：「孟嘗君<u>客</u>我。」

　　車：＿＿＿＿＿＿＿＿＿＿＿＿＿＿＿＿＿＿＿＿＿

　　揭：＿＿＿＿＿＿＿＿＿＿＿＿＿＿＿＿＿＿＿＿＿

　　過：＿＿＿＿＿＿＿＿＿＿＿＿＿＿＿＿＿＿＿＿＿

　　客：＿＿＿＿＿＿＿＿＿＿＿＿＿＿＿＿＿＿＿＿＿

　　整句翻譯：＿＿＿＿＿＿＿＿＿＿＿＿＿＿＿＿＿

　　＿＿＿＿＿＿＿＿＿＿＿＿＿＿＿＿＿＿＿＿＿＿＿

　　＿＿＿＿＿＿＿＿＿＿＿＿＿＿＿＿＿＿＿＿＿＿＿

4. 「責<u>畢</u>收，<u>以</u>何市而<u>反</u>？」孟嘗君曰：「<u>視</u>吾家所寡有者。」

　　畢：＿＿＿＿＿＿＿＿＿＿＿＿＿＿＿＿＿＿＿＿＿

　　以：＿＿＿＿＿＿＿＿＿＿＿＿＿＿＿＿＿＿＿＿＿

　　反：＿＿＿＿＿＿＿＿＿＿＿＿＿＿＿＿＿＿＿＿＿

　　視：＿＿＿＿＿＿＿＿＿＿＿＿＿＿＿＿＿＿＿＿＿

　　整句翻譯：＿＿＿＿＿＿＿＿＿＿＿＿＿＿＿＿＿

　　＿＿＿＿＿＿＿＿＿＿＿＿＿＿＿＿＿＿＿＿＿＿＿

　　＿＿＿＿＿＿＿＿＿＿＿＿＿＿＿＿＿＿＿＿＿＿＿

5. <u>驅</u>而<u>之</u>薛，使吏<u>召</u>諸民當償者，<u>悉</u>來合券。

　　驅：＿＿＿＿＿＿＿＿＿＿＿＿＿＿＿＿＿＿＿＿＿

　　之：＿＿＿＿＿＿＿＿＿＿＿＿＿＿＿＿＿＿＿＿＿

　　召：＿＿＿＿＿＿＿＿＿＿＿＿＿＿＿＿＿＿＿＿＿

　　悉：＿＿＿＿＿＿＿＿＿＿＿＿＿＿＿＿＿＿＿＿＿

整句翻譯：_____

_____

_____

6. 臣<u>竊</u><u>計</u>君宮中<u>積</u>珍寶，狗馬<u>實</u>外<u>廄</u>，美人<u>充</u>下<u>陳</u>。

竊：_____

計：_____

積：_____

實：_____

廄：_____

充：_____

陳：_____

整句翻譯：_____

_____

_____

7. 孟嘗君<u>就</u>國於薛。

就：_____

整句翻譯：_____

_____

_____

8. 先生所為文<u>市</u>義者，<u>乃</u>今日見之。

市：_____

乃：_____

整句翻譯：_____

_____

_____

✎ III. Grammar Exercise

Write down the grammatical function Ⓕ and meaning Ⓔ of the word "為" in the following sentences.

1. 為之駕，比門下之車客。

   Ⓕ _____

   Ⓔ _____

2. 「長鋏歸來乎，無以為家！」

   Ⓕ _____

   Ⓔ _____

3. 左右皆惡之，以為貪而不知足。

   Ⓕ _____

   Ⓔ _____

4. 寡人不敢以先王之臣為臣。

   Ⓕ _____

   Ⓔ _____

22

Selection from the *Zhanguo ce* (No. 3)

二十二.《戰國策・燕策一》：燕昭王收破燕後即位

✎ I. Text Exercise

Fill in the blanks below. Use one Chinese character for each blank.

1. 燕昭王＿＿＿破燕後＿＿＿位，卑＿＿＿厚幣＿＿＿招賢＿＿＿，
   欲＿＿＿以報＿＿＿。＿＿＿往＿＿＿郭隗先生曰：「齊＿＿＿孤
   國之亂＿＿＿襲破燕。孤＿＿＿知燕小力＿＿＿不足＿＿＿報。
   ＿＿＿得賢士＿＿＿共國，以＿＿＿先王之＿＿＿，＿＿＿之願
   也。＿＿＿問以國＿＿＿讎者奈＿＿＿？」

2. 昭王曰：「＿＿＿人將＿＿＿朝而可？」郭隗先生曰：「臣＿＿＿古
   之＿＿＿人，有＿＿＿千金＿＿＿千里馬＿＿＿，三年不能
   ＿＿＿。＿＿＿人言＿＿＿君曰：『請＿＿＿之。』君＿＿＿之。

3. 三月得千＿＿＿＿馬，馬＿＿＿＿死，買＿＿＿＿首五百＿＿＿＿，反

＿＿＿＿報君。君＿＿＿＿怒曰：『所求者＿＿＿＿馬，＿＿＿＿事死馬

＿＿＿＿捐五百金？』」

🖉 II. Grammar Exercise

Fill in the blanks below with particles 於, 焉, or 乎.

1. 天下聞王朝其賢臣，天下之士必趨＿＿＿＿燕矣。

《戰國策・燕策一：燕昭王收破燕後即位》

2. 君不聞大魚＿＿＿＿？網不能止，鉤不能牽，蕩而失水，則螻蟻得

意＿＿＿＿。

《戰國策・齊策一》：靖郭君將城薛

3. 死馬且買之五百金，況生馬＿＿＿＿？

《戰國策・燕策一：燕昭王收破燕後即位》

4. 吾長見笑＿＿＿＿大方之家。

《莊子・秋水》(節)

5. ＿＿＿＿是不能期年，千里之馬至者三。

《戰國策・燕策一：燕昭王收破燕後即位》

6. 隗且見事，況賢＿＿＿＿隗者＿＿＿＿？

《戰國策・燕策一：燕昭王收破燕後即位》

7. 此何遽不為福＿＿＿＿？

寓言：塞翁失馬

8. 有子問＿＿＿＿＿曾子曰：「問喪於夫子＿＿＿＿＿？」

《禮記》選：(甲) 有子之言似夫子

9. 於是＿＿＿＿＿河伯欣然自喜，以天下之美為盡在己。

《莊子‧秋水》(節)

10.孟嘗君問：「馮公有親＿＿＿＿＿？」

《戰國策‧齊策四》：馮諼客孟嘗君

23

Selection from the *Shiji* (No. 1)

二十三.《史記 · 項羽本紀》(節)

✎ **I. Punctuation Exercise**

Put a dot after each sentence.

1. 於是項王乃悲歌忼慨自為詩曰力拔山
兮氣蓋世時不利兮騅不逝騅不逝兮可之
奈何虞兮虞兮奈若何歌數闋美人和
項王泣數行下左右皆泣莫能仰視

2. 江東雖小地方千里眾數十萬人亦足王
也願大王急渡今獨臣有船漢軍至無以
渡

3. 項王乃曰吾聞漢購我頭千金邑萬戶吾
為若德乃自刎而死

✎ II. Text Exercise

Fill in the blanks below. Use one Chinese character for each blank.

1. 項王軍＿＿＿＿垓下，兵＿＿＿＿食盡，漢＿＿＿＿ ＿＿＿＿諸侯兵圍＿＿＿＿數＿＿＿＿。夜＿＿＿＿漢軍＿＿＿＿面＿＿＿＿楚歌，項王＿＿＿＿大＿＿＿＿曰：「漢＿＿＿＿已得楚＿＿＿＿？是＿＿＿＿楚人＿＿＿＿多＿＿＿＿！」

2. 項王笑曰：「天＿＿＿＿亡我，我＿＿＿＿渡＿＿＿＿！＿＿＿＿籍＿＿＿＿江東子弟八千人渡江＿＿＿＿西，今＿＿＿＿一人還，＿＿＿＿江東＿＿＿＿兄憐＿＿＿＿王我，我何＿＿＿＿ ＿＿＿＿見＿＿＿＿？縱彼＿＿＿＿言，籍＿＿＿＿不愧＿＿＿＿心＿＿＿＿？」

3. 吾騎此馬五＿＿＿＿，＿＿＿＿當＿＿＿＿敵，嘗一日＿＿＿＿千里，不忍殺＿＿＿＿，＿＿＿＿賜公！

✎ III. Translation

Write down the meaning of the underlined words and then translate the sentences.

1. 兵少食<u>盡</u>

   盡：＿＿＿＿＿＿＿＿＿＿＿＿＿＿＿＿＿＿＿＿＿＿＿＿＿＿＿

   整句翻譯：＿＿＿＿＿＿＿＿＿＿＿＿＿＿＿＿＿＿＿＿＿＿＿

2. 常<u>幸</u>從

   幸：＿＿＿＿＿＿＿＿＿＿＿＿＿＿＿＿＿＿＿＿＿＿＿＿＿＿＿

整句翻譯：_____

3. 美人和之

　　和：_____

　　整句翻譯：_____

4. 直夜潰圍南出

　　直：_____

　　整句翻譯：_____

5. 騎能屬者百餘人耳

　　屬：_____

　　整句翻譯：_____

6. 田父給曰

　　田父：_____

　　給：_____

　　整句翻譯：_____

7. 項王自度不得脫

　　度：_____

　　整句翻譯：_____

8. 遂霸有天下

　　遂：_____

　　霸：_____

　　整句翻譯：_____

9. 然今卒困於此

    卒：_____

    整句翻譯：_____

10. 期山東為三處

    期：_____

    整句翻譯：_____

11. 項王瞋目而叱之

    瞋：_____

    叱：_____

    整句翻譯：_____

12. 今獨臣有船

    獨：_____

    整句翻譯：_____

13. 縱江東父兄憐而王我

    縱：_____

    王：_____

    整句翻譯：_____

14. 項王身亦被十餘創

    亦：_____

    被：_____

    創：_____

    整句翻譯：_____

15. 吾<u>為</u><u>若</u>德

　　為：＿＿＿＿＿＿＿＿＿＿＿＿＿＿＿＿＿＿

　　若：＿＿＿＿＿＿＿＿＿＿＿＿＿＿＿＿＿＿

　　整句翻譯：＿＿＿＿＿＿＿＿＿＿＿＿＿＿

24

Selection from the *Shiji* (No. 2)

二十四.《史記‧留侯世家》(節)

✎ **I. Text Exercise**

Fill in the blanks below. Use one Chinese character for each blank.

1. 留侯張良＿＿＿＿，＿＿＿＿先韓人＿＿＿＿。

2. 良＿＿＿＿學禮淮陽，東＿＿＿＿倉海君，＿＿＿＿力士，＿＿＿＿鐵椎
   ＿＿＿＿百二十斤。

3. 秦皇帝大＿＿＿＿，＿＿＿＿索天下，求賊急＿＿＿＿，＿＿＿＿張良故
   ＿＿＿＿。良＿＿＿＿更名姓，亡＿＿＿＿下邳。

4. 良＿＿＿＿為取履，＿＿＿＿長跪＿＿＿＿之。父＿＿＿＿足受，笑＿＿＿＿
   去。良殊＿＿＿＿驚，隨＿＿＿＿之。

5. 五日＿＿＿＿明，良＿＿＿＿。父＿＿＿＿先在，怒曰：「＿＿＿＿老人

＿＿＿＿，後，＿＿＿也？」

6. ＿＿＿＿去，無＿＿＿言，＿＿＿＿復見。旦日視＿＿＿＿書，＿＿＿＿太

公兵法＿＿＿＿。良因＿＿＿＿之，常＿＿＿＿誦讀之。

✎ II. Grammar Exercise

Fill in the blanks with personal pronouns 吾, 我, 君, 女, 爾, 若, 寡人, 不穀, or
孺子.

1. 顧謂良曰：「＿＿＿＿下取履！」良鄂然，欲毆之。為其老，彊忍，

下取履。父曰：「履＿＿＿＿！」

2. ＿＿＿＿聞漢購＿＿＿＿頭千金，邑萬户，＿＿＿＿為＿＿＿＿德。

3. ＿＿＿＿處北海，＿＿＿＿處南海，唯是風馬牛不相及也。不虞

＿＿＿＿之涉＿＿＿＿地也，何故？

4. 昔召康公命＿＿＿＿先君大公曰：五侯九伯，＿＿＿＿實征之，以夾

輔周室，賜＿＿＿＿先君履。

5. ＿＿＿＿貢包茅不入，王祭不共，無以縮酒，＿＿＿＿是徵；昭王南

征而不復，＿＿＿＿是問。

6. 項王身亦被十餘創。顧見漢騎司馬呂馬童，曰：「＿＿＿＿非

＿＿＿＿故人乎？」

7. _____可教矣！後五日平明，與_____會此。

8. 齊侯曰：「豈_____是為？先君之好是繼。與_____同好，如何？」

9. _____若以德綏諸侯，誰敢不服。

10. _____見_____，濟北穀城山下黃石，即_____矣。

25

Selection from the *Shiji* (No. 3)

二十五.《史記 · 魏公子列傳》(節)

✎ **I. Punctuation Exercise**

Put a dot after each sentence.

1. 夷受從冠子梁肯為子大不公子敝家貧遺坐攝公子厚客侯以觀十欲賓生欲七請會侯讓年往大夷門不坐嬴之酒迎上侯聞置自公子乃是左公恭士曰公子於是虛載愈隱者監子騎上轡魏門公車直執

2. 枉客公願其見公子中屠生下察市語微侯在客入與其客引車立臣曰公子子久立謂之故倪愈和又過俾顏色生騎亥子侯車朱子

3. 公子行侯生曰晉鄙不授公子兵而復請
之事必危矣臣客屠者朱亥可與俱此人
力士晉鄙聽大善不聽可使擊之於是公
子請朱亥朱亥遂與公子俱公子過謝侯
生

✎ **II. Text Exercise**

Fill in the blanks below. Use one Chinese character for each blank.

1. 當是＿＿＿，魏將相＿＿＿室賓客＿＿＿堂，＿＿＿公子舉
＿＿＿，市人＿＿＿觀公子＿＿＿轡。從＿＿＿皆＿＿＿罵侯生。
侯生＿＿＿公子＿＿＿終不＿＿＿，乃＿＿＿客＿＿＿車。至
＿＿＿，公子＿＿＿侯生坐上＿＿＿，遍＿＿＿賓客，賓客皆
＿＿＿…。侯生＿＿＿為上客…。

2. ＿＿＿雄＿＿＿雌猶＿＿＿分，攻＿＿＿殺＿＿＿何＿＿＿紛？秦
益＿＿＿邯鄲＿＿＿，＿＿＿王＿＿＿救平原＿＿＿。
＿＿＿子為嬴＿＿＿駟馬，執＿＿＿愈＿＿＿意愈＿＿＿。亥為
＿＿＿肆鼓＿＿＿人，＿＿＿乃夷＿＿＿抱關＿＿＿。非＿＿＿慷
慨＿＿＿奇謀，意＿＿＿兼＿＿＿身命＿＿＿。＿＿＿風刎＿＿＿
送公子，七＿＿＿老翁＿＿＿所＿＿＿？

3. 行＿＿＿夷門，＿＿＿侯生，…侯生曰：「公子＿＿＿之矣，老臣

_____能_____。」公子行_____里，…_____引車_____，

_____侯生。侯生_____曰：「臣_____知公子_____還_____。」

4. 侯生曰：「臣_____從，_____不能。請_____公子行_____，以

晉鄙軍之_____，北鄉自_____以_____公子。」公子

_____行。至_____，_____魏王_____代晉_____。晉鄙合

_____，疑_____，…_____無聽。朱亥_____四十斤_____椎，

椎_____晉鄙，公子_____將晉鄙_____…。秦軍_____去…。

公子與侯生_____，_____軍，侯生_____北_____自剄。

✎ **III. Grammar Exercise**

Fill in the blanks below with particles 之, 而, 為, 以, 其, 與, 於, or 者.

1. 嬴聞晉鄙_____兵符常在王臥內，_____如姬最幸，出入王臥

內，力能竊_____。

2. 嬴聞如姬父_____人所殺，…如姬_____公子泣，公子使客斬

_____仇頭，敬進如姬。

3. 公子從_____計，請如姬。如姬果盜晉鄙兵符_____公子。

4. 公子姊_____趙惠文王弟平原君夫人，數遺魏王及公子書，請救

_____魏。

5. 亥＿＿＿＿屠肆鼓刀人，嬴乃夷門抱關＿＿＿＿。

6. 平原君使者冠蓋相屬＿＿＿＿魏。

7. 如姬＿＿＿＿欲＿＿＿＿公子死，無所辭…。公子誠一開口請如姬，
   如姬必許諾…。

8. 公子＿＿＿＿嬴停駟馬，執轡愈恭意愈下。

9. 公子…乃請賓客，約車騎百餘乘，欲赴秦軍，＿＿＿＿趙俱死。

10. …留軍壁鄴，名＿＿＿＿救趙，實持兩端＿＿＿＿觀望。

Selection from the *Shiji* (No. 4)

二十六.《史記‧李將軍列傳》(節)

✎ I. Text Exercise

Fill in the blanks below. Use one Chinese character for each blank.

1. 三人＿＿＿射，＿＿＿中貴人，殺其騎＿＿＿盡。中＿＿＿人
　　＿＿＿廣。廣曰：「是＿＿＿射雕者＿＿＿。」廣＿＿＿遂從百騎
　　＿＿＿馳三人。

2. 廣＿＿＿百騎＿＿＿大恐，欲＿＿＿還走。廣曰：「吾＿＿＿大軍
　　數十里；今如此＿＿＿百騎走，匈奴＿＿＿射我立＿＿＿。今我
　　＿＿＿，匈奴＿＿＿以我為大軍＿＿＿之，必＿＿＿敢擊
　　＿＿＿。」

3. 其騎曰：「虜多＿＿＿近，＿＿＿有急，＿＿＿何？」

4. 是時_____暮，胡兵終_____之，不敢_____。夜半_____，胡

兵_____以為漢有_____軍_____旁欲夜_____之，胡皆_____兵

而去。平_____，李廣_____歸其大軍。

✎ II. Grammar Exercise

Fill in the blanks below with 於, 為, or 見. Then write down the grammatical
function Ⓕ and meaning Ⓔ of the word 於, 為, and 見.

1. 胡兵亦以為漢有伏軍_____旁。(《史記・李將軍列傳》)

    Ⓕ _____

    Ⓔ _____

2. 見廣，以_____誘騎，皆驚，上山陳。(《史記・李將軍列傳》)

    Ⓕ _____

    Ⓔ _____

3. 中貴人將騎數十縱，_____匈奴三人，與戰。(《史記・李將軍列
   傳》)

    Ⓕ _____

    Ⓔ _____

4. 彼虜以我_____走；今皆解鞍以示不走，用堅其意。(《史記・李
   將軍列傳》)

    Ⓕ _____

    Ⓔ _____

5. 孔子過泰山側，有婦人哭＿＿＿＿＿＿墓者而哀。〔《禮記》選：(乙) 苛政猛於虎〕

　　Ⓕ ＿＿＿＿＿＿＿＿＿＿＿＿＿＿＿＿＿＿＿＿＿＿＿＿＿＿＿＿＿＿

　　Ⓔ ＿＿＿＿＿＿＿＿＿＿＿＿＿＿＿＿＿＿＿＿＿＿＿＿＿＿＿＿＿＿

6. 吾長＿＿＿＿＿＿笑於大方之家。〔《莊子·秋水》(節)〕

　　Ⓕ ＿＿＿＿＿＿＿＿＿＿＿＿＿＿＿＿＿＿＿＿＿＿＿＿＿＿＿＿＿＿

　　Ⓔ ＿＿＿＿＿＿＿＿＿＿＿＿＿＿＿＿＿＿＿＿＿＿＿＿＿＿＿＿＿＿

7. 青，取之＿＿＿＿＿＿藍，而青於藍。〔《荀子·勸學》(節)〕

　　Ⓕ ＿＿＿＿＿＿＿＿＿＿＿＿＿＿＿＿＿＿＿＿＿＿＿＿＿＿＿＿＿＿

　　Ⓔ ＿＿＿＿＿＿＿＿＿＿＿＿＿＿＿＿＿＿＿＿＿＿＿＿＿＿＿＿＿＿

8. 兔不可復得，而身＿＿＿＿＿＿宋國笑。(《韓非子·五蠹》)

　　Ⓕ ＿＿＿＿＿＿＿＿＿＿＿＿＿＿＿＿＿＿＿＿＿＿＿＿＿＿＿＿＿＿

　　Ⓔ ＿＿＿＿＿＿＿＿＿＿＿＿＿＿＿＿＿＿＿＿＿＿＿＿＿＿＿＿＿＿

9. 樂羊以有功＿＿＿＿＿＿疑，秦西巴以有罪益信。(《韓非子·說林上》：巧詐不如拙誠)

　　Ⓕ ＿＿＿＿＿＿＿＿＿＿＿＿＿＿＿＿＿＿＿＿＿＿＿＿＿＿＿＿＿＿

　　Ⓔ ＿＿＿＿＿＿＿＿＿＿＿＿＿＿＿＿＿＿＿＿＿＿＿＿＿＿＿＿＿＿

10. 昔者吾舅死＿＿＿＿＿＿虎。〔《禮記》選：(乙) 苛政猛於虎〕

　　Ⓕ ＿＿＿＿＿＿＿＿＿＿＿＿＿＿＿＿＿＿＿＿＿＿＿＿＿＿＿＿＿＿

　　Ⓔ ＿＿＿＿＿＿＿＿＿＿＿＿＿＿＿＿＿＿＿＿＿＿＿＿＿＿＿＿＿＿

11. 匈奴必以我_____大軍誘之。(《史記・李將軍列傳》)

Ⓕ _____

Ⓔ _____

27

Selection from the *Hanshu*

二十七.《漢書・循吏傳》：龔遂傳（節）

✏️ **I. Punctuation Exercise**

Put a dot after each sentence.

1. 渤海左右郡歲飢盜賊並起二千石不能
   禽制上選能治者丞相御史舉遂可用上
   以為渤海太守

2. 遂對曰海瀕遐遠不霑聖化其民困於飢
   寒而吏不恤故使陛下赤子盜弄陛下將安之之
   兵也

3. 上許焉加賜黃金贈遣乘傳至渤海界郡
   聞新太守至發兵以迎遂皆遣還

✎ II. Text Exercise

Fill in the blanks below. Use one Chinese character for each blank.

1. 時遂＿＿＿七十＿＿＿，＿＿＿見，形貌＿＿＿小。宣帝＿＿＿見，不副＿＿＿聞，心內＿＿＿焉，＿＿＿遂曰：「渤海＿＿＿亂，朕＿＿＿憂之。君＿＿＿何＿＿＿息＿＿＿盜賊，以＿＿＿朕意？」

2. 上聞遂＿＿＿，甚＿＿＿，答＿＿＿：「選用＿＿＿良，＿＿＿欲安＿＿＿也。」遂曰：「臣＿＿＿治亂民＿＿＿治亂＿＿＿，不可＿＿＿也；＿＿＿緩之，＿＿＿後可治。臣＿＿＿丞相御史＿＿＿無＿＿＿臣以＿＿＿法，得一切＿＿＿宜從事。」

3. 移書＿＿＿屬縣：「＿＿＿罷逐捕＿＿＿賊吏，＿＿＿持鉏鉤田器＿＿＿皆為＿＿＿民，吏無得＿＿＿，持＿＿＿者＿＿＿為盜賊。」

4. 遂＿＿＿車＿＿＿行至府，郡中＿＿＿然，盜賊＿＿＿皆罷。渤海又＿＿＿劫掠＿＿＿隨，聞遂＿＿＿令，＿＿＿時解散，棄其兵＿＿＿而持＿＿＿鉏。盜賊＿＿＿是悉＿＿＿，民＿＿＿土樂＿＿＿。

━━━━━━━━━━━━ *28* ━━━━━━━━━━━━

Selection from the *Houhanshu* (No. 1)

二十八.《後漢書 · 酷吏列傳》：董宣傳 (節)

✎ I. Text Exercise

Fill in the blanks below. Use one Chinese character for each blank.

1. 宣特徵＿＿＿洛陽＿＿＿。＿＿＿湖陽公主＿＿＿頭白日＿＿＿

   人，＿＿＿匿主＿＿＿，吏＿＿＿能得。＿＿＿主出行，而＿＿＿

   奴驂＿＿＿，宣＿＿＿夏門亭＿＿＿之，＿＿＿駐車＿＿＿馬，

   ＿＿＿刀畫地，大言＿＿＿主之＿＿＿，＿＿＿奴下車，＿＿＿格

   殺＿＿＿。

2. 宣叩＿＿＿曰：「願＿＿＿一言＿＿＿死。」帝曰：「欲＿＿＿

   言？」宣曰：「陛下聖＿＿＿中＿＿＿，而＿＿＿奴殺良＿＿＿，

   ＿＿＿何以＿＿＿天下＿＿＿？臣不＿＿＿箠，請＿＿＿自殺。」

3. ＿＿＿＿是＿＿＿＿擊＿＿＿＿彊，＿＿＿＿不震＿＿＿＿。京師號為

「＿＿＿＿ ＿＿＿＿」，＿＿＿＿之曰：「枹＿＿＿＿不＿＿＿＿董少平。」

✎ II. Translation

Write down the meaning of the underlined words and then translate the sentences.

1. 主<u>即</u><u>還</u>宮<u>訴</u>帝，帝大怒，<u>召</u>宣，欲<u>箠</u>殺之。

即：＿＿＿＿＿＿＿＿＿＿＿＿＿＿＿＿＿＿＿＿＿＿＿＿＿＿＿＿＿

還：＿＿＿＿＿＿＿＿＿＿＿＿＿＿＿＿＿＿＿＿＿＿＿＿＿＿＿＿＿

訴：＿＿＿＿＿＿＿＿＿＿＿＿＿＿＿＿＿＿＿＿＿＿＿＿＿＿＿＿＿

召：＿＿＿＿＿＿＿＿＿＿＿＿＿＿＿＿＿＿＿＿＿＿＿＿＿＿＿＿＿

箠：＿＿＿＿＿＿＿＿＿＿＿＿＿＿＿＿＿＿＿＿＿＿＿＿＿＿＿＿＿

整句翻譯：＿＿＿＿＿＿＿＿＿＿＿＿＿＿＿＿＿＿＿＿＿＿＿＿

＿＿＿＿＿＿＿＿＿＿＿＿＿＿＿＿＿＿＿＿＿＿＿＿＿＿＿＿＿＿＿＿

＿＿＿＿＿＿＿＿＿＿＿＿＿＿＿＿＿＿＿＿＿＿＿＿＿＿＿＿＿＿＿＿

2. 即<u>以</u>頭<u>擊</u><u>楹</u>，流血<u>被</u><u>面</u>。帝<u>令</u>小<u>黃門</u><u>持</u>之，使宣<u>叩頭</u><u>謝</u>主。

以：＿＿＿＿＿＿＿＿＿＿＿＿＿＿＿＿＿＿＿＿＿＿＿＿＿＿＿＿＿

擊：＿＿＿＿＿＿＿＿＿＿＿＿＿＿＿＿＿＿＿＿＿＿＿＿＿＿＿＿＿

楹：＿＿＿＿＿＿＿＿＿＿＿＿＿＿＿＿＿＿＿＿＿＿＿＿＿＿＿＿＿

被：＿＿＿＿＿＿＿＿＿＿＿＿＿＿＿＿＿＿＿＿＿＿＿＿＿＿＿＿＿

面：＿＿＿＿＿＿＿＿＿＿＿＿＿＿＿＿＿＿＿＿＿＿＿＿＿＿＿＿＿

令：＿＿＿＿＿＿＿＿＿＿＿＿＿＿＿＿＿＿＿＿＿＿＿＿＿＿＿＿＿

黃門：_____

持：_____

叩頭：_____

謝：_____

整句翻譯：_____

_____

_____

3. 宣不從，彊使頓之，宣兩手據地，終不肯俯。

從：_____

彊：_____

頓：_____

據：_____

終：_____

俯：_____

整句翻譯：_____

_____

_____

4. 文叔為白衣時，臧亡匿死，吏不敢至門。今為天子，威不能行一令乎？

為：_____

白衣：_____

臧：_____

亡：_____

至：_____

天子：_____

行：_____

令：_____

整句翻譯：_____

_____

_____

Selection from the *Houhanshu* (No. 2)

二十九.《後漢書·南匈奴傳》：昭君(節)

✏️ I. Punctuation Exercise

Put a dot after each sentence.

《後漢書·南匈奴傳》：昭君(節)

呼韓邪臨辭大會帝召五女以示之昭君豐容靚飾光明漢宮顧景裴回竦動左右帝見大驚意欲留之而難失信遂與匈奴生二子及呼韓邪死其前閼氏子代立欲妻之昭君上書求歸成帝敕令從胡俗遂復為後單于閼氏焉

✏️ II. Text Exercise

Fill in the blanks below. Use one Chinese character for each blank.

《後漢書·南匈奴傳》：昭君(節)

1. 昭君字＿＿＿＿＿，南郡人＿＿＿＿＿。＿＿＿＿＿，元帝時＿＿＿＿＿良家＿＿＿＿＿

選入＿＿＿＿＿庭。＿＿＿＿＿呼韓邪來＿＿＿＿＿，帝＿＿＿＿＿以宮女五人

_____之。昭君_____宮數_____不得見御，積_____怨，_____
請掖庭_____求行。

歐陽修：《明妃曲和王介甫作》

2. 胡人以_____馬為_____，射獵_____俗。泉_____草_____無常
_____，鳥_____獸_____爭馳_____。誰_____漢女_____胡
兒？_____沙無_____貌如_____。身_____不_____中國
_____，馬_____自作_____歸曲。推手_____琵卻_____琶，
_____人共_____亦咨_____。_____顏流_____死天_____，
_____琶卻_____來_____家。漢_____爭按_____聲譜，_____
恨已_____聲更_____。纖_____女手_____洞房，學_____琵琶
_____下堂。不_____黃_____出塞_____，_____知此_____能
_____腸？

✎ III. Matching

Which follows which? Read the text again and match up the sentences. Write the
letters on the lines.

王安石：《明妃曲》

1. 明妃初出漢宮時，_____   A. 好在氈城莫相憶。

2. 低佪顧影無顏色，_____   B. 當時枉殺毛延壽。

3. 歸來卻怪丹青手，_____   C. 淚溼春風鬢腳垂。

4. 意態由來畫不成，＿＿＿＿＿　　　　D. 人生失意無南北！

5. 一去心知更不歸，＿＿＿＿＿　　　　E. 尚得君王不自持。

6. 寄聲欲問塞南事，＿＿＿＿＿　　　　F. 只有年年鴻雁飛。

7. 家人萬里傳消息，＿＿＿＿＿　　　　G. 入眼平生幾曾有？

8. 君不見咫尺長門閉阿嬌，＿＿＿＿＿　H. 可憐著盡漢宮衣。

━━━ *30* ━━━

Tao Yuanming: "The Story of the Peach Blossom Stream"

三十. 陶淵明：《桃花源記》

✎ I. Text Exercise

Fill in the blanks below. Use one Chinese character for each blank.

陶淵明：《桃花源記》

1. _____溪行，忘路_____遠近。

2. 復前_____，欲_____其林。林_____水源，_____得一山。山
_____小口，彷彿_____有光，_____舍船，_____口入。

3. 土地_____曠，屋舍儼_____。有_____田、美_____、桑、竹
之_____。阡_____交通，雞_____相_____。_____中往來種
作，男女衣著，_____如外人，黃_____垂_____，並_____然
自_____。

4. 村中＿＿＿＿有此人，＿＿＿＿來問＿＿＿＿。

5. ＿＿＿＿人各復＿＿＿＿至其家，皆出＿＿＿＿食。停數日，辭＿＿＿＿。

6. ＿＿＿＿出，得＿＿＿＿船，便扶＿＿＿＿路，處處＿＿＿＿之。

王維：《桃源行》

7. 漁＿＿＿＿逐水＿＿＿＿山春，＿＿＿＿岸＿＿＿＿花夾＿＿＿＿津。

   坐＿＿＿紅＿＿＿不知＿＿＿，行＿＿＿青＿＿＿不見＿＿＿。

   山＿＿＿＿潛＿＿＿始隈＿＿＿，＿＿＿開＿＿＿望旋平＿＿＿。

   ＿＿＿看一＿＿＿攢雲＿＿＿，＿＿＿入千＿＿＿散花＿＿＿。

8. ＿＿＿＿客初＿＿＿＿漢姓＿＿＿＿，＿＿＿＿人＿＿＿＿改＿＿＿＿衣服。

   居＿＿＿＿共住＿＿＿＿陵源，＿＿＿＿從＿＿＿＿外起田＿＿＿＿。

   月＿＿＿＿松＿＿＿＿房＿＿＿＿靜；＿＿＿＿出雲＿＿＿＿雞犬＿＿＿＿。

   驚＿＿＿＿俗客＿＿＿＿來集，競＿＿＿＿還家＿＿＿＿都邑。

9. ＿＿＿＿明閭＿＿＿＿掃花＿＿＿＿，薄＿＿＿＿漁＿＿＿＿乘＿＿＿＿入。

   初＿＿＿＿避地＿＿＿＿人間，及至＿＿＿＿仙遂不＿＿＿＿。

   峽＿＿＿＿誰知＿＿＿＿人事，世＿＿＿＿遙＿＿＿＿空雲＿＿＿＿。

   ＿＿＿＿疑靈＿＿＿＿難＿＿＿＿見，＿＿＿＿心未＿＿＿＿思鄉＿＿＿＿。

10. ＿＿＿＿＿洞＿＿＿＿＿論＿＿＿＿＿山水，＿＿＿＿＿家終＿＿＿＿＿長＿＿＿＿＿衍。

　　　自＿＿＿＿＿經過＿＿＿＿＿不＿＿＿＿＿，安＿＿＿＿＿峰＿＿＿＿＿今＿＿＿＿＿變。

　　　＿＿＿＿＿時＿＿＿＿＿記入＿＿＿＿＿深，＿＿＿＿＿溪幾＿＿＿＿＿到雲＿＿＿＿＿。

　　　春來＿＿＿＿＿是桃＿＿＿＿＿水，不＿＿＿＿＿仙＿＿＿＿＿何＿＿＿＿＿尋。

✎ II. Grammar Exercise

(1) Fill in the blanks with 不, 無, or 未.

1. 中＿＿＿＿＿＿雜樹，芳草鮮美，落英繽紛。

2. 先世避秦時亂，率妻子邑人來此絕境，＿＿＿＿＿＿復出焉。

3. 乃＿＿＿＿＿＿知有漢，＿＿＿＿＿＿論魏、晉！

4. 此中人語云：「＿＿＿＿＿＿足為外人道也。」

5. 南陽劉子驥，高尚士也，聞之，欣然規往。＿＿＿＿＿＿果，尋病終。

　　後遂＿＿＿＿＿＿問津者。

6. 太守即遣人隨其往，尋向所誌，遂迷＿＿＿＿＿＿復得路。

(2) Write down the characteristics of these negatives.

1. 不：＿＿＿＿＿＿＿＿＿＿＿＿＿＿＿＿＿＿＿＿＿＿＿＿＿＿＿＿＿＿＿＿＿＿＿＿

　　＿＿＿＿＿＿＿＿＿＿＿＿＿＿＿＿＿＿＿＿＿＿＿＿＿＿＿＿＿＿＿＿＿＿＿＿＿＿

2. 無： _____

   _____

3. 未： _____

   _____

(3) Fill in the blanks with 不, 無, or 未.

1. 肉食者鄙，_____能遠謀。

2. 夫子之牆數仞，_____得其門而入，_____見宗廟之美，百官之富。

3. 今吾子愛人則以政，猶_____能操刀而使割也，其傷實多。

4. 失其魂魄，五色_____主。

5. 僑聞學而後入政，_____聞以政學者也。

6. 子路曰：「願車馬衣輕裘與朋友共，敝之而_____憾。」顏淵曰：「_____伐善，_____施勞。」

31

Wang Xizhi: "Preface to the Lanting Gathering"

三十一. 王羲之：《蘭亭集序》

✎ **I. Punctuation Exercise**

Put a dot after each sentence.

永和九年歲在癸丑暮春之初會于會稽山
陰之蘭亭脩禊事也群賢畢至少長咸集此映
地有崇山峻嶺茂林脩竹又有清流激湍絲
帶左右引以為流觴曲水列坐其次雖無情是
竹管絃天朗氣清惠風和暢仰宇宙大俯
日也品類信可樂也一清以游目騁懷足以觀極視聽之
察娛

✎ II. Text Exercise

Fill in the blanks below. Use one Chinese character for each blank.

1. ＿＿＿人之＿＿＿與，俯＿＿＿一世，＿＿＿取諸＿＿＿抱，＿＿＿言一室＿＿＿內，＿＿＿因寄＿＿＿託，放＿＿＿形骸之＿＿＿。

2. ＿＿＿趣舍＿＿＿殊，靜＿＿＿不同，＿＿＿其欣＿＿＿所＿＿＿，＿＿＿得＿＿＿己，快＿＿＿自足，不＿＿＿老＿＿＿將至。

3. 及＿＿＿所之＿＿＿倦，情＿＿＿事＿＿＿，＿＿＿慨係之＿＿＿。向＿＿＿所欣，俛＿＿＿之間，已＿＿＿陳跡，＿＿＿不能＿＿＿以之＿＿＿懷；＿＿＿修短＿＿＿化，＿＿＿期於＿＿＿。古人＿＿＿：「死＿＿＿亦＿＿＿矣。」＿＿＿不痛＿＿＿！

4. ＿＿＿覽昔＿＿＿興感之＿＿＿，若＿＿＿一＿＿＿，＿＿＿嘗不文嗟＿＿＿，不＿＿＿喻之於＿＿＿。

5. ＿＿＿知＿＿＿死生＿＿＿虛誕，＿＿＿彭殤為＿＿＿作，＿＿＿之視＿＿＿，亦＿＿＿今之＿＿＿昔，悲＿＿＿！

6. 故＿＿＿敘＿＿＿人，＿＿＿其＿＿＿述，雖＿＿＿殊＿＿＿異，＿＿＿以＿＿＿懷，＿＿＿致一＿＿＿。後＿＿＿覽＿＿＿，亦＿＿＿有感＿＿＿斯文。

━━━━━━━━━━━━━━━━━━━━ *32* ━━━━━━━━━━━━━━━━━━━━

Han Yu: "Miscellaneous Essays No. 4"

三十二. 韓愈：《雜說四》

✎ I. Text Exercise

Fill in the blanks below. Use one Chinese character for each blank.

1. 世有＿＿＿樂，＿＿＿後有＿＿＿里馬。千里馬＿＿＿有，＿＿＿
   伯樂＿＿＿常有。＿＿＿雖有名馬，祇辱＿＿＿奴隸人＿＿＿
   手，＿＿＿死＿＿＿槽櫪之間，不＿＿＿千里稱＿＿＿。

2. ＿＿＿馬也，＿＿＿有千里之＿＿＿，食不＿＿＿，力不＿＿＿，
   才＿＿＿不＿＿＿見，＿＿＿欲與＿＿＿馬等不＿＿＿得，＿＿＿
   求其能千里＿＿＿。

✎ II. Translation

Translate the following sentences into English.

1. 馬之千里者，一食或盡粟一石。食馬者，不知其能千里而食也。

_____

_____

_____

2. 策之不以其道，食之不能盡其材，鳴之而不能通其意，執策而臨之曰：「天下無馬。」

_____

_____

_____

3. 嗚呼！其真無馬邪？其真不知馬也！

_____

_____

_____

━━━━━━━━━━━━━━━━━━ *33* ━━━━━━━━━━━━━━━━━━━━━━

Han Yu: "On Teachers"

三十三. 韓愈：《師說》

✎ I. Text Exercise

Fill in the blanks below. Use one Chinese character for each blank.

1. 古之＿＿＿者必有＿＿＿。師＿＿＿，＿＿＿以傳＿＿＿、受
   ＿＿＿、解＿＿＿也。

2. 古之＿＿＿人，其＿＿＿人也＿＿＿矣，＿＿＿且從師而問
   ＿＿＿。今之＿＿＿人，其＿＿＿聖人＿＿＿亦遠＿＿＿，而
   ＿＿＿學於師。是故聖＿＿＿聖，愚益＿＿＿，聖人＿＿＿所以
   聖，愚人之＿＿＿以為＿＿＿，其＿＿＿出於＿＿＿乎？

3. 巫、＿＿＿、＿＿＿師，百＿＿＿之人，不＿＿＿相師；士大夫
   之＿＿＿，曰＿＿＿、曰弟子＿＿＿者，＿＿＿群聚而＿＿＿之。
   問之，＿＿＿曰：「彼＿＿＿彼年相＿＿＿也，道相＿＿＿也。」

4. 是＿＿＿＿弟子＿＿＿＿必不＿＿＿＿師，師不必＿＿＿＿於＿＿＿＿子，聞

＿＿＿＿有＿＿＿＿後，＿＿＿＿業有＿＿＿＿攻，如＿＿＿＿而＿＿＿＿。

✎ II. Grammar Exercise (1)

Fill in the blanks below with the words 於, 乎, 吾, 我, 余, 其, 之, 亦, 乃, 而, 則, 也, or 矣.

1. 生＿＿＿＿吾前，其聞道也，固先乎＿＿＿＿，吾從而師之。生乎吾

後，＿＿＿＿聞道也，＿＿＿＿先乎吾，＿＿＿＿從而師之。

2. 愛＿＿＿＿子，擇師＿＿＿＿教之，於其身＿＿＿＿，＿＿＿＿恥師焉，

惑＿＿＿＿！

3. 巫、醫、樂師、百工＿＿＿＿人，君子不齒，今＿＿＿＿智＿＿＿＿反

不能及，＿＿＿＿可怪＿＿＿＿歟？！

4. 位卑＿＿＿＿足羞，官盛＿＿＿＿近諛。嗚呼！師道＿＿＿＿不復可知

＿＿＿＿。

5. 三人行，必有＿＿＿＿師。

6. 不拘＿＿＿＿時，學於＿＿＿＿，＿＿＿＿嘉＿＿＿＿能行古道，作師說

以貽＿＿＿＿。

✎ **III. Grammar Exercise (2)**

(1) Fill in the blanks below with 無, 不, 非, or 未.

1. 人＿＿＿＿生而知之者，孰能＿＿＿＿惑？惑而＿＿＿＿從師，其為惑也，終＿＿＿＿解矣。

2. 是故＿＿＿＿貴＿＿＿＿賤，＿＿＿＿長＿＿＿＿少，道之所存，師之所存也。

3. 嗟乎！師道之＿＿＿＿傳也久矣！欲人之＿＿＿＿惑也難矣！

4. 彼童子之師，授之書而習其句讀者，＿＿＿＿吾所謂傳其道、解其惑者也。句讀之＿＿＿＿知，惑之不解，或師焉，或＿＿＿＿焉，小學而大遺，吾＿＿＿＿見其明也。

5. 聖人＿＿＿＿常師。

(2) Write down the features of these negative particles.

1. 無：＿＿＿＿＿＿＿＿＿＿＿＿＿＿＿＿＿＿＿＿＿＿＿＿＿＿＿＿＿＿＿＿＿

＿＿＿＿＿＿＿＿＿＿＿＿＿＿＿＿＿＿＿＿＿＿＿＿＿＿＿＿＿＿＿＿＿

2. 不：＿＿＿＿＿＿＿＿＿＿＿＿＿＿＿＿＿＿＿＿＿＿＿＿＿＿＿＿＿＿＿＿＿

＿＿＿＿＿＿＿＿＿＿＿＿＿＿＿＿＿＿＿＿＿＿＿＿＿＿＿＿＿＿＿＿＿

3. 非：＿＿＿＿＿＿＿＿＿＿＿＿＿＿＿＿＿＿＿＿＿＿＿＿＿＿＿＿＿＿＿＿＿

＿＿＿＿＿＿＿＿＿＿＿＿＿＿＿＿＿＿＿＿＿＿＿＿＿＿＿＿＿＿＿＿＿

4. 未：＿＿＿＿＿＿＿＿＿＿＿＿＿＿＿＿＿＿＿＿＿＿＿＿＿＿＿＿＿＿＿＿＿

＿＿＿＿＿＿＿＿＿＿＿＿＿＿＿＿＿＿＿＿＿＿＿＿＿＿＿＿＿＿＿＿＿

━━━━━━━━━━━━━━━━━━ *34* ━━━━━━━━━━━━━━━━━━

Liu Zongyuan: "The Donkey from Qian"

三十四. 柳宗元：《黔之驢》

✏️ **I. Text Exercise**

Fill in the blanks below. Use one Chinese character for each blank.

1. 黔＿＿＿驢，有＿＿＿＿事者，船載＿＿＿＿入；至＿＿＿＿無可用，
   放＿＿＿＿山下。虎＿＿＿＿之，龐＿＿＿＿大物＿＿＿＿，以＿＿＿＿神。

2. ＿＿＿＿日，驢一＿＿＿＿，虎大＿＿＿＿，遠＿＿＿＿，以為＿＿＿＿噬己
   ＿＿＿＿，甚＿＿＿＿！

3. 虎＿＿＿＿喜，＿＿＿＿之曰：「＿＿＿＿止此＿＿＿＿！」＿＿＿＿跳踉大
   ＿＿＿＿，＿＿＿＿其喉，盡＿＿＿＿肉，＿＿＿＿去。

II. Translation

Please translate the following sentences into English.

1. 蔽林間窺之，稍出近之，慭慭然莫相知。

2. 然往來視之，覺無異能者，益習其聲，又近出前後，終不敢搏。

3. 稍近益狎，蕩倚衝冒。驢不勝怒，蹄之。

4. 向不出其技，虎雖猛，疑畏卒不敢取，今若是焉，悲夫！

✎ III. Grammar Exercise

Fill in the blanks below to complete the exclamatory expressions. Then write down the meaning or feature of these exclamations.

1. _____！形之龐也，類有德，聲之宏也，類有能。

   _____

2. 今若是焉，悲_____！

   _____

3. _____ _____！師道之不傳也久矣！

   _____

4. _____ _____！師道之不復可知矣。

   _____

35

Liu Zongyuan: "A Note on the Xiaoshicheng Hill"

三十五. 柳宗元：《小石城山記》

✎ I. Text Exercise

Fill in the blanks below. Use one Chinese character for each blank.

1. ＿＿＿西山＿＿＿口徑北，＿＿＿黃茅嶺＿＿＿下，＿＿＿二道：＿＿＿一西出，尋之無＿＿＿得。其一少北＿＿＿東，＿＿＿過四十丈，＿＿＿斷而川＿＿＿，有＿＿＿石橫＿＿＿其垠。

2. 其上＿＿＿睥＿＿＿梁欐之＿＿＿，其＿＿＿出堡＿＿＿，有＿＿＿門＿＿＿，窺＿＿＿正黑。投＿＿＿小石，洞＿＿＿有水聲。其響＿＿＿激越，良久＿＿＿已。環之＿＿＿上，望＿＿＿遠。

3. ＿＿＿土壤＿＿＿生＿＿＿樹美箭，＿＿＿奇＿＿＿堅。其＿＿＿數偃＿＿＿，＿＿＿智者＿＿＿施設也。

4. ＿＿＿＿！＿＿＿＿疑造物＿＿＿＿之有＿＿＿＿久矣。＿＿＿＿是愈以為

＿＿＿＿有。又＿＿＿＿其不＿＿＿＿之中州，＿＿＿＿列是夷＿＿＿＿，更

千百年＿＿＿＿得一售＿＿＿＿伎，是＿＿＿＿勞＿＿＿＿無用，神＿＿＿＿

償不宜＿＿＿＿是，＿＿＿＿其果無＿＿＿＿？

✎ II. Grammar Exercise

Fill in the blanks below to complete these passive voice sentences. Then translate these sentences into English.

1. 或曰：「以慰夫賢而辱＿＿＿＿此者。」

＿＿＿＿＿＿＿＿＿＿＿＿＿＿＿＿＿＿＿＿＿＿＿＿＿＿＿＿＿＿

＿＿＿＿＿＿＿＿＿＿＿＿＿＿＿＿＿＿＿＿＿＿＿＿＿＿＿＿＿＿

2. 吾長＿＿＿＿笑＿＿＿＿大方之家。

＿＿＿＿＿＿＿＿＿＿＿＿＿＿＿＿＿＿＿＿＿＿＿＿＿＿＿＿＿＿

＿＿＿＿＿＿＿＿＿＿＿＿＿＿＿＿＿＿＿＿＿＿＿＿＿＿＿＿＿＿

3. 青，取之＿＿＿＿藍，而青於藍。

＿＿＿＿＿＿＿＿＿＿＿＿＿＿＿＿＿＿＿＿＿＿＿＿＿＿＿＿＿＿

＿＿＿＿＿＿＿＿＿＿＿＿＿＿＿＿＿＿＿＿＿＿＿＿＿＿＿＿＿＿

4. 兔不可復得而身＿＿＿＿宋國笑。

＿＿＿＿＿＿＿＿＿＿＿＿＿＿＿＿＿＿＿＿＿＿＿＿＿＿＿＿＿＿

＿＿＿＿＿＿＿＿＿＿＿＿＿＿＿＿＿＿＿＿＿＿＿＿＿＿＿＿＿＿

5. 樂羊以有功＿＿＿＿疑，秦西巴以有罪益信。

＿＿＿＿＿＿＿＿＿＿＿＿＿＿＿＿＿＿＿＿＿＿＿＿＿＿＿＿＿＿

＿＿＿＿＿＿＿＿＿＿＿＿＿＿＿＿＿＿＿＿＿＿＿＿＿＿＿＿＿＿

36

Bo Juyi: "The Song of the Pipa" with the Preface

三十六. 白居易：《琵琶行》并序

✎ I. Punctuation Exercise

Put a dot after each sentence.

元和十年予左遷九江郡司馬明年秋送客湓浦口聞舟中夜彈琵琶者聽其音錚錚然有京都聲問其人本長安倡女嘗學琵琶於穆曹二善才年長色衰委身為賈人婦遂命酒使快彈數曲曲罷憫然自敘少小時歡樂事今漂淪自歌以贈之凡六百一十六言命曰琵琶行恬然為琶

✎ II. Text Exercise

Fill in the blanks below. Use one Chinese character for each blank.

1. 轉_____撥絃_____兩_____，未成_____調先有_____；絃
_____掩抑聲聲_____，似_____平生_____得意。

2. 閒_____鶯_____花底_____，幽_____泉流_____下_____；水
_____冷澀絃_____絕，凝絕不_____聲暫_____。

3. _____罷曾_____善才服，_____成每_____秋娘_____；武陵
_____少爭_____頭，一_____紅綃不知_____；鈿_____銀篦
節碎，血_____羅裙_____酒_____。

4. 老大_____作商人_____！商人_____利輕_____別，前_____浮
梁買_____去；去來_____口守_____船，_____船月明江水
_____。夜_____忽夢少年_____，_____啼妝淚_____闌干。

5. 我_____琵琶已_____息，又聞_____語_____唧唧！_____是天
_____淪_____人，_____逢何_____曾相_____！

6. 今夜_____君琵琶_____，_____聽仙_____耳暫明。_____辭更
坐_____一曲，_____君翻_____琵琶_____。

III. Rearrangement

Rearrange the following sentences in the correct order.

1. 潯江頭送夜客陽/，/花瑟葉荻楓秋瑟/。/主客船下馬在人/，/絃酒欲飲管舉無/；/不將醉歡成慘別/，/時江茫浸別月茫/。

---

2. 邀船見相近相移/，/回添燈開重酒宴/。/始千萬喚出呼來/，/面琵猶半琶遮抱/。

---

3. 攏慢抹輕復挑撚/，/為初霓後六裳么/。/急絃嘈如嘈雨大/，/小語切如切私絃/，/切嘈錯切雜嘈彈/，/盤珠大小落珠玉/。

---

4. 言感我此久立良/，/絃卻促絃轉急坐/；/淒不前似向聲淒/，/滿重泣聞掩座/。/中泣最下誰多座/？/衫州江司青溼馬/。

37

Fan Zhongyan: "A Note on the Yueyang Pavilion"

三十七. 范仲淹：《岳陽樓記》

✎ **I. Text Exercise**

Fill in the blanks below. Use one Chinese character for each blank.

1. 慶_____四年春，滕子京_____守巴陵_____。_____明年，政
   _____人_____，百廢_____興，_____重修岳陽_____，_____
   其舊_____，_____唐賢_____人詩賦_____其上；_____予作文
   _____記之。

2. _____夫霪_____霏霏，_____月不開；陰風_____號，濁浪
   _____空；日_____隱耀，山岳_____形；商旅_____行，檣傾
   _____摧，薄暮_____冥，虎_____猿_____；登_____樓
   _____，則有_____國懷鄉，憂_____畏譏，滿目_____然，感
   _____而悲_____矣！

3. 嗟＿＿＿！＿＿＿嘗求＿＿＿仁人＿＿＿心，或＿＿＿二者之
＿＿＿，何＿＿＿？不＿＿＿物＿＿＿，＿＿＿以＿＿＿悲，
＿＿＿廟堂＿＿＿高，＿＿＿憂＿＿＿民；＿＿＿江湖＿＿＿遠，
＿＿＿憂其＿＿＿。＿＿＿進＿＿＿憂，退＿＿＿憂；然則＿＿＿
時而樂＿＿＿？其＿＿＿曰：「＿＿＿天下＿＿＿憂＿＿＿憂，
＿＿＿天下＿＿＿樂而樂＿＿＿？」＿＿＿！＿＿＿斯人，吾
＿＿＿與歸！＿＿＿六年九月十五日。

✎ II. Grammar Exercise

Fill in the blanks below. Use only one Chinese character for each blank. Then, write down the meaning of these particles.

1. 野語有之曰：「聞道百，以為莫己若」者，我之謂也。＿＿＿
＿＿＿我嘗聞少仲尼之聞，而輕伯夷之義者。〔《莊子・秋水》
（節）〕

_____

_____

2. 匠石曰：「臣則嘗能斲之，＿＿＿＿＿＿，臣之質死久矣。」〔《莊
子・徐無鬼》：運斤成風（節）〕

_____

_____

3. ＿＿＿＿＿ ＿＿＿＿＿北通巫峽，南極瀟湘，遷客騷人，多會於此。(《岳陽樓記》)

＿＿＿＿＿＿＿＿＿＿＿＿＿＿＿＿＿＿＿＿＿＿＿＿＿＿＿＿＿＿＿＿＿

＿＿＿＿＿＿＿＿＿＿＿＿＿＿＿＿＿＿＿＿＿＿＿＿＿＿＿＿＿＿＿＿＿

4. 是進亦憂，退亦憂；＿＿＿＿＿ ＿＿＿＿＿何時而樂耶？(《岳陽樓記》)

＿＿＿＿＿＿＿＿＿＿＿＿＿＿＿＿＿＿＿＿＿＿＿＿＿＿＿＿＿＿＿＿＿

＿＿＿＿＿＿＿＿＿＿＿＿＿＿＿＿＿＿＿＿＿＿＿＿＿＿＿＿＿＿＿＿＿

5. ＿＿＿＿＿ ＿＿＿＿＿霪雨霏霏，連月不開；陰風怒號，濁浪排空。(《岳陽樓記》)

＿＿＿＿＿＿＿＿＿＿＿＿＿＿＿＿＿＿＿＿＿＿＿＿＿＿＿＿＿＿＿＿＿

＿＿＿＿＿＿＿＿＿＿＿＿＿＿＿＿＿＿＿＿＿＿＿＿＿＿＿＿＿＿＿＿＿

6. ＿＿＿＿＿ ＿＿＿＿＿春和景明，波瀾不驚，上下天光，一碧萬頃。(《岳陽樓記》)

＿＿＿＿＿＿＿＿＿＿＿＿＿＿＿＿＿＿＿＿＿＿＿＿＿＿＿＿＿＿＿＿＿

＿＿＿＿＿＿＿＿＿＿＿＿＿＿＿＿＿＿＿＿＿＿＿＿＿＿＿＿＿＿＿＿＿

38

Ouyang Xiu: "A Note on the Zuiweng Pavilion"

三十八. 歐陽修：《醉翁亭記》

✎ **I. Text Exercise**

Fill in the blanks below. Use one Chinese character for each blank.

1. 山＿＿＿＿六七里，漸＿＿＿＿水聲＿＿＿＿潺，而＿＿＿＿出於兩＿＿＿＿
   之間者，＿＿＿＿泉也。峰回＿＿＿＿轉，有亭＿＿＿＿然臨於＿＿＿＿
   上者，醉翁＿＿＿＿也。作亭＿＿＿＿誰？山之＿＿＿＿智僊也。
   ＿＿＿＿之者＿＿＿＿？太守＿＿＿＿謂＿＿＿＿。

2. 宴＿＿＿＿之樂，＿＿＿＿絲＿＿＿＿竹，射者＿＿＿＿，弈者＿＿＿＿，
   ＿＿＿＿籌交＿＿＿＿，起坐而＿＿＿＿譁者，眾賓＿＿＿＿也。＿＿＿＿顏
   ＿＿＿＿髮，＿＿＿＿然＿＿＿＿其間者，太守＿＿＿＿也。

3. ＿＿＿＿而夕陽＿＿＿＿山，＿＿＿＿影散亂，太守＿＿＿＿而賓客＿＿＿＿

也。樹林陰＿＿＿＿，鳴＿＿＿＿上下，遊人＿＿＿＿而禽鳥＿＿＿＿

也。＿＿＿＿而禽＿＿＿＿知山林＿＿＿＿樂，＿＿＿＿不＿＿＿＿人之

樂。

✎ II. Grammar Exercise

Fill in the blanks below with the words provided.

1. 環滁皆山＿＿＿＿。＿＿＿＿西南諸峰，林壑尤美。望＿＿＿＿蔚然
   ＿＿＿＿深秀＿＿＿＿，瑯琊＿＿＿＿。

   （其／者／之／也／而）

2. 若＿＿＿＿日出＿＿＿＿林霏開，雲歸＿＿＿＿巖穴暝，晦明變化
   ＿＿＿＿，山間＿＿＿＿朝暮＿＿＿＿。野芳發＿＿＿＿幽香，佳木秀
   ＿＿＿＿繁陰，風霜高潔，水落＿＿＿＿石出＿＿＿＿，山間＿＿＿＿四
   時＿＿＿＿。朝＿＿＿＿往，暮＿＿＿＿歸，四時＿＿＿＿景不同，＿＿＿＿
   樂亦無窮＿＿＿＿。

   （而／者／之／也／夫）

3. 太守＿＿＿＿客來飲＿＿＿＿此，飲少輒醉，而年又最高，＿＿＿＿自
   號曰「醉翁」＿＿＿＿。醉翁之意＿＿＿＿在酒，在＿＿＿＿山水之間
   ＿＿＿＿。山水＿＿＿＿樂，得＿＿＿＿心而寓之酒＿＿＿＿。

   （於／乎／與／不／之／故／也）

4. 人知_____太守遊而樂，_____不知太守_____樂_____樂也。醉能同_____樂，醒能述_____文_____，太守_____。太守謂_____？廬陵歐陽修_____。

(誰／從／也／其／者／之／而)

5. 臨谿_____漁，谿深_____魚肥；釀泉_____酒，泉香_____酒列；山肴野蔌，雜然_____前陳_____，太守宴_____。

(而／者／為／也)

━━━━━━━━━━━━━━ 39 ━━━━━━━━━━━━━━

Wang Anshi: "A Note on My Visit to Mt. Baochan"

三十九. 王安石：《遊褒禪山記》

✎ I. Text Exercise

Fill in the blanks below. Use one Chinese character for each blank.

1. _____是予有歎_____。古人之_____於天地、_____川、_____
   木、_____魚、_____獸，往_____有得，以其求_____之深而
   _____不在也。

2. 夫_____以近，_____遊者眾；險_____遠，則至_____少。而
   世_____奇偉_____怪非常之_____，常在於_____遠，而人之
   _____罕至焉。_____非有_____者不能至也。

3. 有志_____，不隨_____止也，_____力不足者，亦不_____至
   也。有志_____力，_____又不隨以_____，至於_____暗昏
   惑，而_____物以_____之，_____不能至也。

4. 然力＿＿＿以至＿＿＿而不至，於人＿＿＿可譏，而＿＿＿己為
有悔。＿＿＿吾志也，而不能至＿＿＿，可以無悔＿＿＿。其
＿＿＿能譏之乎？此＿＿＿之所得也！

5. 余＿＿＿仆碑，又以＿＿＿夫古書之不＿＿＿，後世之＿＿＿其
傳而＿＿＿能名者，何可勝道也＿＿＿？此＿＿＿以學者不
＿＿＿以不深思＿＿＿慎取之＿＿＿。

✎ II. Consolidation Exercise (Adverbs)

Fill in the blanks with the following adverbs.

時間副詞：始，卒，今，將，且，遂，業，已，既，嘗，時，忽，
初，尋，先，後，終，即，向，乃，因

程度副詞：甚，愈，極，尤

性態副詞：亦，猶，尚，又，必，誠，固，殊，復，相

範圍副詞：各，具，俱，悉，咸，並，皆

Then, write down the meaning of these adverbs.

歐陽修：《醉翁亭記》

1. 環滁＿①＿山也。其西南諸峰，林壑＿②＿美。

① ＿＿＿＿＿＿＿＿＿＿＿＿＿＿＿＿＿＿＿＿＿＿＿＿＿＿

② ＿＿＿＿＿＿＿＿＿＿＿＿＿＿＿＿＿＿＿＿＿＿＿＿＿＿

王安石：《遊褒禪山記》

2. 褒禪山，＿＿①＿＿謂之華山。唐浮圖慧褒＿＿②＿＿舍於其址，而＿＿③＿＿葬之，以故其後名之曰褒禪。＿＿④＿＿所謂慧空禪院者，褒之廬冢也。

① _____

② _____

③ _____

④ _____

3. 距洞百餘步，有碑仆道，其文漫滅，＿＿①＿＿其為文＿＿②＿＿可識，曰：「花山。」＿＿③＿＿言「華」如「華實」之「華」者，蓋音謬也。

① _____

② _____

③ _____

4. 其下平曠，有泉側出，而記遊者＿＿①＿＿眾，所謂前洞也。由山以上五六里，有穴窈然，入之＿＿②＿＿寒，問其深，則其好遊者不能窮也，謂之後洞。

① _____

② _____

5. 予與四人擁火以入，入之＿＿①＿＿深，其進＿②＿難，而其見
＿＿③＿＿奇。有怠而出者，曰：「不出，火＿④＿盡。」＿⑤＿與之
＿＿⑥＿＿出。

① _____

② _____

③ _____

④ _____

⑤ _____

⑥ _____

6. 蓋予所至，比好遊者＿＿①＿＿不能十一，然視其左右，來而記之者
＿②＿少。蓋其＿＿③＿＿深，則其至＿④＿加少矣。

① _____

② _____

③ _____

④ _____

7. 方是時，予之力＿＿①＿＿足以入，火＿＿②＿＿足以明也。＿③＿其
出，則或咎其欲出者，而予＿④＿悔其隨之，而不得極乎遊之樂
也。

① _____

② _____

③
_____

④
_____

范仲淹:《岳陽樓記》

8. 嗟夫!予___①___求古仁人之心,或異二者之為,何哉?

①
_____

9. 其___①___曰:「先天下之憂而憂,後天下之樂而樂歟?」

①
_____

柳宗元:《小石城山記》

10. 無土壤而生嘉樹美箭,___①___奇而堅。

①
_____

11. 噫!吾疑造物者之有無久矣。及是___①___以為___②___有。

①
_____

②
_____

柳宗元:《黔之驢》

12. 他日,驢一鳴,虎大駭,遠遁,以為___①___噬己也,___②___恐!

①
_____

②
_____

13. ____①____ 不出其技，虎雖猛，疑畏____②____ 不敢取，____③____若是焉，悲夫！

① _____

② _____

③ _____

陶淵明：《桃花源記》

14. ____①____逢桃花林，夾岸數百步，中無雜樹，芳草鮮美，落英繽紛。

① _____

15. 其中往來種作，男女衣著，____①____如外人，黃髮垂髫，____②____怡然自樂。

① _____

② _____

16. 見漁人，乃大驚，問所從來；____①____答之。

① _____

17. 村中聞有此人，____①____來問訊。

① _____

18. 餘人____①____復延至其家，____②____出酒食。

　　① ＿＿＿＿＿＿＿＿＿＿＿＿＿＿＿＿＿＿＿＿＿＿＿＿＿＿＿

　　② ＿＿＿＿＿＿＿＿＿＿＿＿＿＿＿＿＿＿＿＿＿＿＿＿＿＿＿

19. ____①____出，得其船，便扶向路，處處誌之。

　　① ＿＿＿＿＿＿＿＿＿＿＿＿＿＿＿＿＿＿＿＿＿＿＿＿＿＿＿

20. 太守____①____遣人隨其往，尋____②____所誌，遂迷不____③____得路。

　　① ＿＿＿＿＿＿＿＿＿＿＿＿＿＿＿＿＿＿＿＿＿＿＿＿＿＿＿

　　② ＿＿＿＿＿＿＿＿＿＿＿＿＿＿＿＿＿＿＿＿＿＿＿＿＿＿＿

　　③ ＿＿＿＿＿＿＿＿＿＿＿＿＿＿＿＿＿＿＿＿＿＿＿＿＿＿＿

21. 未果，____①____病終。____②____遂無問津者。

　　① ＿＿＿＿＿＿＿＿＿＿＿＿＿＿＿＿＿＿＿＿＿＿＿＿＿＿＿

　　② ＿＿＿＿＿＿＿＿＿＿＿＿＿＿＿＿＿＿＿＿＿＿＿＿＿＿＿

寓言選（上）：（丁）畫蛇添足

22. 舍人____①____謂曰。

　　① ＿＿＿＿＿＿＿＿＿＿＿＿＿＿＿＿＿＿＿＿＿＿＿＿＿＿＿

23. 一人蛇____①____成，引酒____②____飲之，____③____左手持卮，右手畫蛇曰。

　　① ＿＿＿＿＿＿＿＿＿＿＿＿＿＿＿＿＿＿＿＿＿＿＿＿＿＿＿

②
_____

③
_____

24.「蛇　①　無足，子安能為之足？」　②　飲其酒。為蛇足者，
　　　③　亡其酒。

①
_____

②
_____

③
_____

《史記・留侯世家》(節)

25. 良　①　為取履，　②　長跪履之。

①
_____

②
_____

26. 五日平明，良往。父　①　先在。

①
_____

27. 良　①　大驚，隨目之。父去里所，　②　還。

①
_____

②
_____

《戰國策・齊策四》：馮諼客孟嘗君

28. 臣竊矯君命，以責賜諸民，　①　燒其券，民稱萬歲。

① _____

29. 先生所為文市義者，____①____ 今日見之。

① _____

《左傳‧莊公十年》：曹劌論戰

30. 十年春，齊師伐我。公____①____ 戰，曹劌請見。

① _____

Su Shi: "On the Marquis of Liu"

四十. 蘇軾：《留侯論》

✎ **I. Text Exercise**

Fill in the blanks below. Use one Chinese character for each blank.

1. 古之＿＿＿＿謂豪＿＿＿＿之士＿＿＿＿，必有＿＿＿＿人之節。人情
＿＿＿＿所不能忍＿＿＿＿，匹夫＿＿＿＿辱，拔劍＿＿＿＿起，＿＿＿＿身
而鬥，＿＿＿＿不足＿＿＿＿勇也。天下有＿＿＿＿勇者，卒＿＿＿＿臨
之＿＿＿＿不驚，無＿＿＿＿加之而不＿＿＿＿，此＿＿＿＿所挾持者
＿＿＿＿大，而其＿＿＿＿甚遠也。

2. ＿＿＿＿子房受＿＿＿＿於圯上＿＿＿＿老人也，＿＿＿＿事＿＿＿＿怪；
＿＿＿＿亦＿＿＿＿知其非秦＿＿＿＿世，有隱君子＿＿＿＿，出而＿＿＿＿
之。＿＿＿＿其所以＿＿＿＿見其意＿＿＿＿，＿＿＿＿聖賢相＿＿＿＿警戒

之義；＿＿＿＿世不察，以＿＿＿＿鬼物，＿＿＿＿已＿＿＿＿矣。且＿＿＿＿意不＿＿＿＿書。

3. ＿＿＿＿韓之亡，秦之＿＿＿＿盛也，以＿＿＿＿鋸鼎＿＿＿＿待天下之＿＿＿＿。＿＿＿＿平居＿＿＿＿罪夷滅＿＿＿＿，不可＿＿＿＿數。＿＿＿＿有賁、育，無＿＿＿＿復施。＿＿＿＿持法＿＿＿＿急者，其＿＿＿＿不可＿＿＿＿，而其末可＿＿＿＿。子房不＿＿＿＿忿＿＿＿＿之心，＿＿＿＿匹夫之力＿＿＿＿逞於一＿＿＿＿之間，＿＿＿＿此之時，子房之不死＿＿＿＿，其＿＿＿＿不能容＿＿＿＿，＿＿＿＿亦已危＿＿＿＿。

✎ II. Grammar Exercise

Fill in the blanks with particles 之, 於, 以, 為, 何, 所, 者, 也, 其, 而, 此, 然, or 故.

千金＿＿＿＿子不死＿＿＿＿盜賊。＿＿＿＿者？＿＿＿＿身之可愛，＿＿＿＿盜賊之不足＿＿＿＿死也。子房＿＿＿＿蓋世之材，不＿＿＿＿伊尹、太公之謀，而特出＿＿＿＿荊軻、聶政之計，＿＿＿＿僥倖於不死，＿＿＿＿圯上老人之＿＿＿＿為深惜＿＿＿＿也。是＿＿＿＿倨傲鮮腆而深折＿＿＿＿，彼＿＿＿＿能有所忍也，＿＿＿＿後可以就大事，＿＿＿＿曰：「孺子可教＿＿＿＿。」

✎ III. Consolidation Exercise (Negatives)

(1) Please write down the features of the following negatives.

1. 不：_____

2. 弗：_____

3. 未：_____

4. 無：_____

5. 非：_____

6. 莫：_____

7. 勿：_____

8. 微：_____

(2) Fill in the blanks with the above negatives.

1. 然亦安知其_____秦之世，有隱君子者，出而試之。

2. 夫子之牆數仞，_____得其門而入，_____見宗廟之美，百官之富。得其門者或寡矣。夫子之云，_____亦宜乎？

3. 己所不欲，_____施於人。

4. 公曰：「衣食所安，_____敢專也，必以分人。」對曰：「小惠_____偏，民_____從也。」

5. 當韓之亡，秦之方盛也，以刀鋸鼎鑊待天下之士。其平居_____
   罪夷滅者，_____可勝數。雖有賁、育，_____所復施。

6. _____斯人，吾誰與歸！

7. 是葉公_____好龍也，好夫似龍而_____龍者也。

8. 失其魂魄，五色_____主。

9. 天下_____柔弱於水，而攻堅強者_____之能勝，以其_____以
   易之。

10. _____成，一人之蛇成，奪其卮曰。